Big Book of
Cupcakes

presented by **Southern Living**

Big Book of Cupcakes

150 brilliantly delicious dreamcakes

by **Jan Moon**

Oxmoor House

ISBN-13: 978-0-8487-3437-4
ISBN-10: 0-8487-3437-8
Library of Congress Control Number: 2010936025

Printed in the United States of America
First Printing 2011

To order additional publications, call 1-800-765-6400 or 1-800-491-0551.

For more books to enrich your life, visit **oxmoorhouse.com**

To search, savor, and share thousands of recipes, visit **myrecipes.com**

Cover: Mocha Latte (page 88), Chocolate-Chocolate Chunk (page 82), Sweet Lavender Cupcakes (page 122), Lemon Love (page 56), Old Glory (page 110)
Back Cover: Sand Dollars (page 121), Peaches-and-Cream (page 113), Over the Moon (page 37), Under the Big Top (page 32)

Oxmoor House
VP, Publishing Director: Jim Childs
Editorial Director: Susan Payne Dobbs
Brand Manager: Daniel Fagan
Managing Editor: Laurie S. Herr

Big Book of Cupcakes
Senior Editor: Rebecca Brennan
Project Editor: Georgia Dodge
Senior Designer: Melissa Jones Clark
Assistant Designer: Allison L. Sperando
Director, Test Kitchens: Elizabeth Tyler Austin
Assistant Directors, Test Kitchens: Julie Christopher, Julie Gunter
Test Kitchens Professionals: Wendy Ball, Allison E. Cox, Victoria E. Cox, Margaret Monroe Dickey, Alyson Moreland Haynes, Callie Nash, Kathleen Royal Phillips, Catherine Crowell Steele, Leah Van Deren
Photography Director: Jim Bathie
Senior Photo Stylist: Kay E. Clarke
Associate Photo Stylist: Katherine Eckert Coyne
Assistant Photo Stylist: Mary Louise Menendez
Production Managers: Theresa Beste-Farley, Tamara Nall Wilder

Contributors
Author: Jan Moon
Copy Editors: Donna Baldone, Carmine B. Loper
Proofreader: Adrienne S. Davis
Indexer: Mary Ann Laurens
Photographer: Becky Luigart-Stayner
Photo Stylist: Jan Gautro
Food Stylist: Katie Moon
Interns: Christine T. Boatwright, Caitlin Watzke

contents

Introduction

"A dream is a wish your heart makes..."
                                    Cinderella

Dreamcakes Bakery is a dream I've had since I was old enough to bake. My obsession with baking began when Santa brought my oldest sister, Linda, an Easy-Bake Oven for Christmas. I was 5 years old. It was all fascinating—combining the ingredients to make a soft sweet batter, pouring it into the shiny miniature pans, placing it into the tiny oven, and then watching and waiting while it magically transformed into cake! Everyday at Dreamcakes we transform all kinds of batter into sweet treats. The process is still magical to me even today. The rhythm of the oven doors opening and closing. The hum of the mixers. The sweet aroma of chocolate, strawberry, and caramelized sugar. It's all still so exciting!

By the time I was 12 and allowed to bake on my own, like any good Southern girl, I turned to *Southern Living* magazine as the go-to resource for good food. I was always the first to read it. I would sit on our front porch poring over all the possibilities. It never disappointed. And the beautiful images inside each issue made it even more enticing to create. Of course I was always attracted to the cakes and pastries. I thought the greatest job on earth would be to work there.

After college, because the headquarters for
Southern Living was practically down the street, I soon found my dream of working there coming true. I pestered Vanessa Johnson, the Test Kitchens Director at that time, until she finally gave up and gave me a job; we are still best friends today. Working in the Test Kitchens became my real education. It was like being in culinary school for 15 years. I especially loved being a food stylist. I learned that you truly taste with your eyes first, so making food beautiful is as important as making it taste good. I still believe this to be true; nothing goes out of our store or into our case without every attention to detail being addressed—sometimes to the extreme. We have a saying that some things worth doing are worth overdoing, but only with the best ingredients and intentions.

My passion for cake decorating
started when my children Ben, Katie, and Jackson came along. I hated the deception of store-bought cakes; they looked so pretty, but lacked the depth of flavor I desired. I wanted so desperately to create beautiful cakes. My sister Linda sent me $25 to take a cake decorating class because at that time we had to watch every penny we earned. There was no extra; it was a choice of groceries or the class. Today when I think of this, it still makes me so aware that you never know where such a small investment in someone will lead—that $25 changed my life. I try whenever I can to invest in people and their dreams.

I learned that you truly taste with your eyes first, so making food beautiful is as important as making it taste good.

Dreamcakes Bakery was a dream held captive in my heart. I talked about it so much that people would tire of hearing about how one day I was going to open my own shop, but they didn't see me taking that leap of faith. Vowing in exhaustion, with my fist raised like Scarlett O'Hara in *Gone with the Wind,* to never have my kitchen floor covered in cake crumbs, powdered sugar, or icing ever again, I found our first location. A truly miniature kitchen (only appropriate I think) in a sleepy little community called Cahaba Heights just outside of Birmingham, Alabama. It was about 300 square feet and had a window unit air conditioner from the 1970s. We had a calculator and a cash box that we kept in the warming drawer of the oven. For me it was as exciting as when the Easy-Bake Oven arrived that Christmas so long ago. The dream was now a reality. Those first few months were euphoric. My daughter Katie came to work with me. We bought a small pastry case and began to fill it with cupcakes that today are still our best sellers. We named them for music we love (I once listened to Katie play Madonna on her iPod everyday for a week), beloved literary characters, and artists. Red Velvet became "Just Because" for just because it's your birthday or just because it's Valentine's Day. "Over the Moon," our signature cupcake, evolved from a plain white vanilla bean cupcake to one with a marbled sky blue frosting topped with white chocolate and edible glitter; we began to sell out everyday.

Within 6 months, we outgrew our little shop. We could barely keep up with the demand. If you could have been a fly on the wall, what you heard would have sounded like siblings in their mother's kitchen. We laugh so much that I'm sure our customers wonder about us sometimes. We soon moved to Edgewood, a Mayberry-like community also on the outskirts of Birmingham, to a shop with 10 times the space; honest to goodness real air conditioning; and a full-size bakery case big enough to hold more than a dozen flavors at once, along with our other specialties. We bake in small batches, so everything is fresh; most days we sell out, and then it all starts over. This limits how much we can sell, but we aren't willing to sacrifice quality for quantity.

We are purists when it comes to ingredients; we are persnickety about 3 things—the flavor, the presentation, and the consistency. It all has to be done in excellence or not at all. The testing process can be tedious: We all have to agree before the product makes it out to our customers. We won't sell anything that we wouldn't take home ourselves. The only exception is that Katie hates cinnamon and raisins, so we let her abstain from those because she will never agree to anything with them in it (we all just roll our eyes).

The changing seasons set the pace for our bakery. We love holidays and celebrations of any kind. It's a joy that we get to share in so many happy occasions. This book is a reflection of how Dreamcakes' menu changes each spring, summer, fall, and winter. You'll see in many recipes how we like to incorporate seasonal ingredients, buying from local farmers as much as possible. You'll also find included in this book some creative ways to display our cupcakes that we hope will inspire your own designs.

Jan Moon

Our motto is:

"Cupcakes Make People Happy," so in our small way, we strive to make people happy everyday. We hope this cookbook will bring you happiness as well.

Cupcakes 101

Making cupcakes is an adventure well worth the effort. It requires only the most basic equipment and a few key ingredients to get started. When unsure of how to proceed, I have a friend who will say, "Just pick a place and start." I think that's splendid advice!

There is nothing more satisfying than seeing the smile on someone's face as they take their first bite of a Dreamcakes cupcake. We make them radical with delicious flavors; they're like gourmet desserts wrapped in small packages. Combine frosted cake, art, and music, and you get a dreamcake. But first, let's get down to basics. Grab your apron and mixer, and let's get started.

Cupcakes 101

The Basics: *tools and equipment*

First things first—be sure you have the proper equipment. You probably already have most everything you need right in your cupboard.

Baking Pans: This is one item where you get what you pay for. Investing in good-quality pans pays off with great cupcakes, and they'll last for many years. We use three sizes at Dreamcakes: miniature, regular (or standard), and jumbo. If you choose nonstick or dark pans, reduce your oven temperature by 25°. Keep in mind: Most of the recipes in this book will make about 24 regular cupcakes, 48 mini cupcakes, or 18 jumbo cupcakes. Pan sizes differ, so be aware your yield can vary. Remember to fill cups two-thirds full except when noted otherwise.

Candy Thermometer: This tool gives accurate temperature readings when making caramel and syrups used for frostings.

Cooling Racks: Racks help cupcakes cool quickly and uniformly. They also can be placed inside a baking sheet to help catch drips when glazing and finishing cupcakes.

Food Processor: This appliance makes quick and easy work of pureeing fruit and chopping large quantities of foods, such as nuts and carrots.

Ice Cream Scoops: We use these to fill pans with batter. They're convenient and give an accurate measurement yielding consistent size and even baking times. Scoops come in three sizes—miniature, regular, and jumbo.

Baking Pan Sizes:

- Each cup of a **miniature-size** muffin pan holds 2 tablespoons of batter. Bake time is approximately 10 to 12 minutes.

- Each cup of a **regular-size** muffin pan holds scant ½ cup of batter. Bake time is approximately 12 to 15 minutes.

- Each cup of a **jumbo-size** muffin pan holds scant 1 cup of batter. Bake time is approximately 18 to 22 minutes.

Immersion Blender: This is one of my most favorite tools! It makes quick work of blending and pureeing ingredients such as fruits and sauces with no fuss.

Measuring Cups and Measuring Spoons: You will need liquid and dry measuring cups and graduated measuring spoons for accurate measuring of ingredients. Baking is a science and requires precision.

Mixer: A good stand mixer makes the job so much easier. With a stand mixer you can gradually add ingredients while the mixer is running and consistently control the speed. A heavy-duty hand mixer will also work and is great for mixing small batches.

Mixing Bowls: You'll need all sizes. The different sizes are great for keeping ingredients organized and separated to be combined later, for melting butter and chocolate, and for mixing colored frostings and fillings.

Pastry Brushes: Brushes are handy for applying glazes.

Sifter: A small, hand-held, fine sifter/sieve is used for sifting powdered sugar, spices, and cocoa over the tops of cupcakes with an even, uniform dusting.

Timers and Testers: One of the greatest causes of failure in baking is overbaking. A good timer and cake tester will be invaluable in knowing when your cupcakes are ready. Always start with the lowest bake time. You can always add more time, but you can't fix a burned cupcake. Ovens differ in how they bake, so until you know if your oven bakes fast or slow, keep a close watch to get the best results. If you are unsure, a wooden skewer or thin metal cake tester inserted in the center of a cupcake is the best way to test for doneness. It should come out clean or with only a few moist crumbs.

Wooden Spoons: These are great when stirring hot ingredients such as caramel because the handles remain cool.

Zester and Channel Knife: The sharp holes in the zester easily (see photo, page 14) remove the zest from lemons and other citrus fruits and produce a fine, fluffy product. The channel knife makes long strips of zest for decorations and garnishes.

Spatulas: We use all sizes of spatulas at the bakery for folding, scraping, and blending. Offset spatulas work particularly well for spreading and smoothing frosting. The angle of the offset design allows you to keep your hands from getting in the frosting. They are also valuable in removing or loosening cupcakes from the pan.

Tips and Techniques:
bake like a pro

Read and Assemble: Always read completely through the recipe before getting started. Assemble and measure all of your ingredients ahead of time to be sure you have everything you need and that it's all fresh.

Soft and Smooth: Make sure butter is softened before you begin. Letting it stand at room temperature about 30 minutes usually does the trick.

Plan Ahead: Preheat your oven for 10 minutes before you're ready to bake.

Be Exact: Carefully measure ingredients—measuring correctly is vital when baking. Use an ice cream scoop to evenly portion the batter.

Better Butter: Browning butter enhances its rich flavor. To brown butter, melt butter in a heavy saucepan over medium heat, stirring frequently, until butter just begins to turn a delicate golden brown color. (Butter will bubble and foam. WATCH CLOSELY.) Immediately remove from heat, and pour into a bowl to cool.

Full Flavor: Take the time to toast nuts and coconut. It really brings out the depths of their flavors.

Easy Does It: Don't overmix your batter; stir only until dry ingredients are incorporated or you will end up with tough cupcakes.

Simple Scooping: Spray ice cream scoops with cooking spray before scooping batter, and the batter will come out cleanly.

Prevent Overflows: Be sure to never fill cups more than two-thirds full unless a recipe specifically instructs it.

Timing is Everything: Place pans on the center rack of your oven, and rotate halfway through the baking process to ensure even baking. Check frequently, and avoid overbaking.

Frosting Pointers: • When preparing frostings and fillings, your ingredients should be at room temperature. • After all ingredients are incorporated, continue to beat frosting a couple of minutes. It makes a light, creamy frosting and improves spreading consistency. • You may have to adjust ingredient amounts slightly to attain the correct consistency. Add liquid, 1 tablespoon at a time, if your frosting is too thick to spread or pipe. Add more powdered sugar, 3 to 4 tablespoons at a time, if your frosting is too thin. • Most frosting will keep for 1 week stored in the refrigerator in airtight containers. For best results, re-whip before using. • Cupcakes with perishable frosting, like cream cheese frosting, need to be stored in the refrigerator.

Cupcake Liners: These keep you from having to grease and flour the baking pan and make removal and decorating easier. We find the foil or heavy-duty, grease-proof liners work the best. You can find paper baking cups in a wide array of fun colors and designs that add a nice touch to any celebration. Be aware, however, that thin paper liners tend to fade and lose their pizzazz once baked.

Special Touches:
dusting, filling, and glazing

Delicate dustings, surprise fillings, and decadent glazes add layers of flavor to cupcakes.

How-To Dust: Using a small hand-held, fine sifter/sieve, gently dust powdered sugar, cocoa, and spices over the tops of your cupcakes.

How-To Fill: To fill cupcakes, insert the end of a wooden spoon or dowel into the center of the cupcake to make a hole. Fill a zip-top plastic freezer bag with filling or frosting. Use scissors or kitchen shears to snip about ¼ inch from one corner of bag; insert bag into the hole in the cupcake. Squeeze gently until filling comes to the top of each cupcake. **Note:** If you want to fill *and* frost 1 recipe of cupcakes with the same frosting, you will need about 6 cups of frosting total.

How-To Glaze: With a spoon, slowly pour glaze over cupcake starting at the center. Repeat until desired amount of glaze covers the cupcake.

Frosting and Piping:
practice makes perfect

There are two ways to frost a cupcake—piping using a decorating bag and tip and frosting by hand.

Zip-top Plastic Freezer Bags: These are wonderful for loading cupcakes with fillings or topping with frosting. Be sure to use the freezer-style bags because they are sturdy enough to hold up to pressure while squeezing.

Decorating/Piping Bags: Decorating bags are cone-shaped bags to which you can attach or insert a metal piping tip for decorating with frosting and for piping whipped cream and other fillings. There are many varieties, but we prefer the disposable heavy-duty ones.

Piping Tips: Tips come in a variety of sizes and shapes. We use round tips and star tips in all sizes depending on the desired design. Use a plain, round tip to outline details, fill in areas, write messages, and create string work, beads, dots, stems, vines, lattices, and scrolls. Use a star tip to pipe large swirls of frosting on top of the cupcakes. The larger the tip, the bigger the swirl.

How-To Pipe a Swirl: Measure and cut a small hole at the end of the decorating bag—only the end of the tip should come through the opening. Twist the open end of the bag to seal contents. Fit the decorating bag with a large star tip. Fill bag half full with frosting. Starting at center of cupcake, and holding the bag at a 90° angle, pipe a star of frosting. Without releasing pressure, move piping bag to the right, and pipe frosting in a clockwise motion, piping close to edge and making a complete circle. Repeat process for a taller swirl of frosting.

How-To Frost by Hand: Place a heaping spoonful of frosting in center of cupcake. With an offset spatula, push frosting to edges while turning cupcake. Rotate cupcake, and lift the frosting with the spatula to create peaks.

Stocking the Pantry: *ingredients*

Baking Soda and Baking Powder: Both baking soda and baking powder are leavening agents; they are added to the batter before baking to produce carbon dioxide which causes the cupcake to rise. When using baking soda, the reaction begins as soon as the ingredients are mixed, so you need to bake these recipes immediately or they will fall. Also, check the expiration date to be sure the ingredient is fresh or your batter won't rise.

Baking powder contains baking soda, but it also includes an acid (such as cream of tartar) and a drying agent. You can substitute baking powder in place of baking soda (you'll need more baking powder, which may affect the flavor), but you can't use baking soda in place of baking powder. Baking soda alone lacks the acidity to make the baked good rise; it is used in recipes that have other acidic ingredients such as buttermilk and chocolate. If needed, you can make your own baking powder by mixing two parts cream of tartar with one part baking soda.

Butter and Shortening: Don't even think about using margarine. Butter makes a far superior batter. Shortening gives a tender, soft crumb and helps retain structure, while butter adds flavor.

Melting Chocolate:

To microwave: Place chocolate in a microwave-safe bowl, set power to MEDIUM (50% power), and heat, stirring occasionally, 1 to 2 minutes or until melted per 4 to 6 ounces.

Over direct heat: Place chocolate in heavy-duty saucepan over very low heat until melted, stirring occasionally. Do not cover the pan. Chocolate scorches easily, so watch it carefully.

Over hot water: Melt chocolate slowly in a double boiler or in a bowl placed over a pan of hot water. Be careful not to get water into the chocolate because the chocolate will clump or harden (seize).

Chocolate: Chocolate used for baking comes in many forms—bars, morsels, chips, chunks, unsweetened cocoa powder, and melted. Do not substitute chocolate syrup for melted chocolate in any recipe. We also don't recommend buying chocolate that is already melted.

Cocoa: This is one ingredient on which you don't want to skimp. Buy the best quality available with the highest fat content for excellent flavor and texture. Unsweetened cocoa results when the cocoa solids leftover from pressing the cocoa butter out of chocolate liquor are dried and ground into powder. Unsweetened cocoa can be natural or dutched. Dutch process cocoa gives a nice smooth flavor with no bitter aftertaste; it has been treated with an alkali to help neutralize chocolate's natural acidity creating a richer, darker product than regular unsweetened cocoa. Do not substitute instant cocoa mix for unsweetened cocoa.

Coconut: Coconut is sold fresh and processed (processed coconut is sold in cans or bags). You will find it sweetened or unsweetened. It comes shredded, flaked, and grated, and it comes at room temperature or frozen. Any variety you choose will work in our recipes. Toasting coconut enhances the flavor and colors it a very light golden brown. To toast coconut, spread it in a single layer on a baking sheet with shallow sides. Bake at 325°, tossing occasionally, for about 10 minutes.

Cream: Whipping cream is almost all we use in making our frostings. (It doesn't have to be heavy cream.) There is just no substitute for the flavor and texture that cream gives to frostings.

Eggs: All of our recipes call for large eggs. To quickly warm eggs just removed from the refrigerator, let them stand in a bowl of lukewarm water for about 5 minutes.

Flavorings and Extracts: These highly concentrated forms of flavoring are important ingredients in producing a flavorful cupcake. We use several different kinds for batters, frostings, and fillings. If you buy a high-quality extract, a little will go a long way and will save you money in the long term.

Flours: I use White Lily flour, an all-purpose soft-wheat flour very similar to cake flour. It produces a light, tender cupcake. All flour should be stored in an airtight container. If flour is stored in the refrigerator, it should be brought to room temperature before using.

Stir flour in the bag or canister with a large spoon to loosen it. Lightly spoon flour into a dry measuring cup, and level with a spatula or knife. Be careful not to tap or shake the measuring cup while measuring. It's not necessary to sift the flour when baking unless the recipe specifically states to do so.

Food Colorings: At Dreamcakes we use highly concentrated food coloring gel. It produces vibrant color using very small amounts. We begin by adding one drop at a time to tint frosting until we reach the desired color. One tip to remember is that colored frosting becomes darker as it dries, so start with one shade lighter if you are using pastel colors.

Fruits: When using fresh fruits in baking, the riper the better. The flavor is fully developed and comes through. If the fruit we want for a recipe is out of season, we prefer to use preserves and jams. Frozen fruit can add unwanted liquid.

Milk and Buttermilk: These are the standard liquids we use in most of our batters.

Stir-ins: In some of our recipes you'll see stir-ins such as nuts, fruits, colorings, or flavorings. If there is something you don't like or don't want to use, simply leave it out or substitute your own stir-in.

Sugars: Use granulated sugar or castor (superfine) sugar for cake batters. The 10X powdered sugar is best for making frostings and glazes. And we consistently buy dark brown sugar for recipes because of the rich, deep flavor it gives, but you can substitute light brown sugar.

Specialty Flour:

Gluten-Free: Gluten-free baked goods taste best when eaten the same day they are made; they do freeze well if you're making them ahead. Gluten-free flours may require more leavening to compensate for their lack of elasticity. If you convert a recipe to gluten-free, you may need to add about 25% more baking soda or baking powder than what is called for in the original version. To prevent clumping that can occur when you use gluten-free flours, whisk dry ingredients in a separate bowl before combining with other ingredients.

Finishing Flair: *decorations*

Candies and Toppings: A few of the toppings we use are candied fruit slices, bite-size cookies, chocolate-covered malted milk balls, Sixlets®, candy berries, Nerds®, M&Ms®, gumballs, jelly beans, Jordan almonds, crumbled toffee, peppermint bits, and chocolate curls.

Colored Sugar and Sparkling Sugar: Find colored sugar on the baking aisle, or make your own by adding food coloring to granulated sugar. Sparkling sugar is a large, coarse-grained sugar that adds sparkle.

Edible Glitter: This flavorless glitter adds a pretty edible sparkle to all of your baked goods. Be sure to use only glitter that is marked "edible."

Edible Glitter Stars: This glitter is sparkle in star form. It comes in silver and gold and makes a really special presentation. Again, be sure to use only glitter stars that are marked "edible."

Fresh Flowers: Fresh flowers are a lovely way to top a cupcake. Although many are edible, you may not really want to eat them. Be sure to use nonpoisonous flowers grown without pesticides. See page 90 for more information on choosing edible flowers.

Gum Paste and Sugar Flowers: These are flowers made from a sugar dough that dries hard. They are edible, but you don't really want to eat them; they add beauty but are flavorless.

Luster Spray: This pearlized food spray adds luster and shine to frostings; make sure it's labeled edible. Apply a light application of spray after frosting and decorating.

Molded Sugar Pieces: Options include dogs, cats, and other animals, footballs, tools, lips, carrots, bees, trains, baby shower decorations, and skulls. The pieces provide a quick, playful way to give a professional look to your cupcakes.

Novelties: Some fancy additions to cupcakes include tiaras, wands, king cake babies, wedding rings, champagne flutes, and glass slippers. Think outside the box. The party favor aisle is a great place to start. Most craft, hobby, and dollar stores have great selections to choose from. Since novelties sometimes look like candy, make sure everyone, especially children, understands they're for decoration only.

Picks: Decorative picks are a fun topper that can personalize cupcakes; they come in an endless choice of themes and colors. You can find incredibly creative handmade ones at etsy.com or at crafts and party stores.

Sprinkles, Dragées, and Pearls: These decorations come in a variety of colors and sizes. Some dragées and other decorative toppings are marked "for decoration only" so be sure to select only those labeled as edible; otherwise, make sure everyone, especially children, understands to remove them before eating.

To Decorate Edges: Place a generous amount of colored sugar or other decorating candy in the palm of your hand or in a shallow bowl. Hold the cupcake at an angle, and gently roll the edges in the candy to coat.

Spring Fever

Springtime down South is a splendid feast for the eyes. It is grand inspiration for the fabulous flavors of spring that we love. Springtime is when we showcase some of Dreamcakes' most loved favorites. It is the perfect place to begin the dream...

Wedding Cake is without a doubt the bestselling cupcake at Dreamcakes. It's the cupcake that started it all. I have used this cake for my wedding cakes for 20 years. There is just something about the combination of flavors and possibly the memories it evokes from weddings or grandmother's kitchen that keeps this flavor sensation at the top of the list.

Wedding Cake

makes 24 cupcakes

1   recipe White Cake (page 32)
2   recipes Wedding Cake Frosting

Toppings: white sparkling sugar, gum paste roses, edible pearl candies

1. Prepare White Cake as directed.
2. Fill each cupcake with Wedding Cake Frosting. (See How-To, page 21.)
3. Frost each cupcake with Wedding Cake Frosting using metal tip no. 2D. (See How-To, page 23.) Top each with sparkling sugar, gum paste roses, and edible pearls.

wedding cake frosting

½   cup butter, softened
¼   cup whipping cream
½   tsp. almond extract
⅛   tsp. salt
1   (16-oz.) package powdered sugar

1. Beat first 4 ingredients at medium speed with an electric mixer until creamy.
2. Gradually add powdered sugar, beating at low speed until blended. Beat at high speed 2 minutes or until creamy. Makes 3 cups.

flip it!

Sweet Proposal

• Turn the Wedding Cake cupcake into an all-important-question cupcake. Spread a smooth layer of Wedding Cake Frosting on the Wedding Cake cupcake. Omit the sugar, rose, and pearl candy toppings; top instead with a set of tiny wedding rings. Tint Wedding Cake Frosting blue with liquid food coloring. Using blue frosting and metal tip no. 3, pipe "Marry me?" onto cupcake.

Bright colors and circus animals are guaranteed to make kids of all ages smile and to make any day a celebration.

Under the Big Top

makes 24 cupcakes

1   recipe White Cake
Multicolored confetti sprinkles
1   recipe Vanilla Frosting

Food coloring gel in your favorite
    colors
Sugar circus animals

1. Prepare White Cake batter; stir in ⅓ cup multicolored confetti sprinkles. Bake as directed; cool as directed.

2. Tint Vanilla Frosting with food coloring gels of your choice. Frost each cupcake with tinted frosting. (See How-To, page 23.) Roll edges of each cupcake in confetti sprinkles, and top each with 1 sugar circus animal.

white cake

½   cup butter, softened
1   cup shortening
2   cups sugar
4   large eggs
2¾ cups all-purpose soft-wheat
    flour
2   tsp. baking powder

½   tsp. salt
1   cup buttermilk
1½ tsp. vanilla extract
1½ tsp. almond extract
Paper baking cups
Vegetable cooking spray

1. Preheat oven to 350°.

2. Beat butter and shortening at medium speed with an electric mixer until creamy; gradually add sugar, beating well. Add eggs, 1 at a time, beating until blended after each addition.

3. Combine flour, baking powder, and salt; add to butter mixture alternately with buttermilk, beginning and ending with flour mixture. Beat at low speed until blended after each addition. Stir in extracts.

4. Place paper baking cups in 2 (12-cup) muffin pans, and coat with cooking spray; spoon batter into cups, filling two-thirds full.

flip it!

Birthday Wishes

• Make a birthday party extra special by turning Under the Big Top cupcakes into colorful party fare. Tint the frosting green. Using metal tip no. 2D, pipe frosting on each cupcake. After frosting the cupcakes, sprinkle multi-colored jimmies around the edge of each cupcake to make a festive border. Instead of circus animals, pierce gumballs with decorative picks and insert one pick into the center of each cupcake.

baker's secret

• Check out your local crafts store or look online at cakedeco.com to buy sugar circus animals.

5. Bake for 12 to 15 minutes or until a wooden pick inserted in center comes out clean. Cool in pans on wire racks 10 minutes; remove from pans to wire racks, and cool completely. **Makes 24 cupcakes.**

vanilla frosting

½	cup butter, softened	⅛	tsp. salt
3	to 4 Tbsp. whipping cream	1	(16-oz.) package powdered
1	tsp. clear vanilla extract		sugar

1. Beat first 4 ingredients at medium speed with an electric mixer until creamy.

2. Gradually add powdered sugar, beating at low speed until blended. Beat at high speed 2 minutes or until creamy. **Makes 3 cups.**

Ultimate comfort food...the blend of pureed strawberries and sweet cream is a soda fountain favorite. Topped off with a bright red berry candy and striped straw, this cupcake is irresistibly cute. Shake some up, and everyone will twist and shout for more.

Strawberry Milkshake

makes 24 cupcakes

1   recipe Strawberry Cake
1   recipe Vanilla Frosting (page 33)
2   cups Strawberry Frosting (page 42)
2   cups Cream Cheese Frosting

Toppings: red berry candies, red striped drinking straws cut into 3 inch pieces

1. Prepare Strawberry Cake as directed.

2. Fill each cupcake with Vanilla Frosting. (See How-To, page 21.)

3. Stir Strawberry Frosting and Cream Cheese Frosting together gently until marbled. Frost each cupcake with strawberry–cream cheese frosting using metal tip no. 2D. (See How-To, page 23.) Top each with 1 red berry candy and 1 (3-inch) section of a plastic drinking straw. (Remove the straw before eating the cupcake.)

strawberry cake

12 oz. frozen sliced strawberries in syrup, thawed
1   cup butter, softened
1½ cups sugar
4   large eggs
2¾ cups all-purpose soft-wheat flour
2   tsp. baking powder
¼   tsp. baking soda
¼   tsp. salt
2   tsp. strawberry extract
¼   tsp. red liquid food coloring
Paper baking cups
Vegetable cooking spray

1. Preheat oven to 350°.

2. Process strawberries and syrup in a blender or food processor until smooth and pureed.

3. Beat butter and sugar at medium speed with an electric mixer in a large bowl until creamy. Add 1½ cups strawberry puree; beat 1 minute. Add eggs, 1 at a time, beating until blended after each addition.

4. Combine flour, baking powder, baking soda, and salt; add to butter mixture, beating until blended. Stir in strawberry extract and food coloring.

5. Place paper baking cups in 2 (12-cup) muffin pans, and coat with cooking spray; spoon batter into cups, filling two-thirds full.

6. Bake for 12 to 15 minutes or until a wooden pick inserted in center comes out clean. Cool in pans on wire racks 10 minutes; remove from pans to wire racks, and cool completely. **Makes 24 cupcakes.**

Note: Cake flour may be substituted for the all-purpose soft-wheat flour.

cream cheese frosting

½	cup butter, softened	2	(16-oz.) packages powdered
1	(8-oz.) package cream cheese,		sugar
	softened	¼	tsp. salt

1. Beat butter and cream cheese at medium speed with an electric mixer until creamy.

2. Gradually add powdered sugar and salt, beating at low speed until blended. Beat at high speed 2 minutes or until creamy. **Makes about 5 cups.**

flip it!

Simply Strawberry

• Not in the mood for a milkshake? Simply prepare the Strawberry Milkshake recipe as directed, omitting the straw and berry candy. Dress the cupcake with a drizzle of melted strawberry jam.

If there is a rival to Wedding Cake, it is our Over the Moon cupcake. We make it with an oh-so-rich vanilla bean paste that gives it an "out of this world" flavor. One customer said that it tastes like it was kissed by an angel.

Over the Moon

makes 24 cupcakes

1	recipe White Cake (page 32)	Toppings: white chocolate curls,
2	recipes Vanilla Bean Frosting	edible glitter stars
2	drops blue liquid food coloring	

1. Prepare White Cake as directed.

2. Fill each cupcake with Vanilla Bean Frosting. (See How-To, page 21.)

3. Add food coloring to remaining Vanilla Bean Frosting. Stir gently until marbled.

4. Frost each cupcake with marbled frosting using metal tip no. 2D. (See How-To, page 23.) Top each with white chocolate curls and edible glitter stars.

Note: Be sure the container for the glitter stars clearly states that the product is edible.

vanilla bean frosting

½	cup butter, softened	⅛	tsp. salt
¼	cup whipping cream	1	(16-oz.) package powdered
1	tsp. vanilla bean paste		sugar

1. Beat first 4 ingredients at medium speed with an electric mixer until creamy.

2. Gradually add powdered sugar, beating at low speed until blended. Beat at high speed 2 minutes or until creamy. **Makes 3 cups.**

Note: We tested with Neilsen-Massey for the vanilla bean paste.

flip it!

Bridesmaid Cupcakes

• With a simple decorating twist, Over the Moon cupcakes make perfect place cards for a Brides-maids' Luncheon. To flip this look, prepare White Cake as directed. Frost cupcakes smooth with the blue Vanilla Bean Frosting. Use metal tip no. 3 and Vanilla Frosting (page 33) to pipe each bridesmaid's monogram on their cupcake.

"Sometimes you feel like a nut, sometimes you don't." Here's where we get our fix for one of our favorite candy bars. For all you chocolate lovers, you might want to keep the chocolate close by for a little extra fix.

Nutty for Coconut

makes 24 cupcakes

1	recipe White Cake (page 32)	Toppings: shredded sweetened
1	recipe Coconut Cream Frosting	coconut, Chocolate Ganache, toasted almonds

1. Prepare White Cake as directed.

2. Fill each cupcake with Coconut Cream Frosting. (See How-To, page 21.)

3. Frost each cupcake with Coconut Cream Frosting. (See How-To, page 23.) Top each with a sprinkle of coconut, a drizzle of Chocolate Ganache, and 2 toasted almonds.

coconut cream frosting

1	cup butter, softened	2	(16-oz.) packages powdered sugar
½	cup cream of coconut	¼	tsp. salt

1. Beat butter and cream of coconut at low speed with an electric mixer until blended.

2. Gradually add powdered sugar and salt, beating at low speed until blended. Beat at high speed 2 minutes or until creamy. **Makes 6 cups.**

Note: We tested with Coco Real cream of coconut.

---

flip it!

Coconut Cream

• For the times you don't "feel like a nut," prepare this recipe as directed, omitting the almonds and Chocolate Ganache. It's a simple Coconut Cream dream!

baker's secret

• Be sure to purchase high-quality chocolate for the ganache. The higher the quality, the better the resulting product.

chocolate ganache

| 1 | cup whipping cream | 8 | oz. semisweet chocolate, chopped |

1. Cook cream in a heavy nonaluminum saucepan over medium heat, stirring often, just until it begins to steam (do not boil); remove from heat.
2. Place chocolate in a glass bowl. Slowly add hot cream to chocolate, beating with a whisk until chocolate melts and mixture is well blended. The mixture will thicken as it cools. **Makes about 2 cups.**

We celebrate birthdays everyday at Dreamcakes! We even keep candles and birthday hats on hand for the occasions. Our buttery cake and chocolate frosting is the perfect way to celebrate anytime.

Birthday Cake

makes 24 cupcakes

1   recipe Butter Cake
1   recipe Chocolate Frosting

Toppings: colored confetti sprinkles, birthday candles

1. Prepare Butter Cake as directed.

2. Frost each cupcake with Chocolate Frosting using metal tip no. 2D. (See How-To, page 23.) Top each with confetti sprinkles and 1 birthday candle.

butter cake

½   cup butter, softened
¾   cup sugar
2   large eggs
1½   cups all-purpose soft-wheat flour
1½   tsp. baking powder
½   tsp. salt
½   cup milk
1   tsp. vanilla extract
Paper baking cups
Vegetable cooking spray

1. Preheat oven to 350°.

2. Beat butter and sugar at medium speed with an electric mixer until creamy. Add eggs, 1 at a time, beating until blended after each addition.

3. Combine flour, baking powder, and salt; add to butter mixture alternately with milk, beginning and ending with flour mixture. Beat at low speed until blended after each addition. Stir in vanilla.

4. Place paper baking cups in 2 (12-cup) muffin pans, and coat with cooking spray; spoon batter into cups, filling two-thirds full.

5. Bake for 12 to 15 minutes or until a wooden pick inserted in center comes out clean. Cool in pans on wire racks 10 minutes; remove from pans to wire racks, and cool completely. **Makes 24 cupcakes.**

flip it!

Make it Special

• This is the perfect recipe for little cakes that will make any day special. Prepare the Butter Cake as directed. Prepare Vanilla Frosting (page 33), and use food coloring to tint it the desired color. Frost each cupcake, and scatter jumbo sprinkles on top. Finish with an extra-tall candle because candles are always fun, even if it's not your birthday!

chocolate frosting

½	cup butter, softened	⅛	tsp. salt
½	cup unsweetened cocoa	1	(16-oz.) package powdered
⅓	cup whipping cream		sugar

1. Beat first 4 ingredients at medium speed with an electric mixer until creamy.

2. Gradually add powdered sugar, beating at low speed until blended. Beat at high speed 2 minutes or until creamy. Makes 3 cups.

Mother's Day Cupcakes are a tradition at Dreamcakes. We love to make anything that is a tribute to our moms. We also call it The Message Cupcake; you can write your own message for any occasion or just to say "I love you."

Mother's Day Cupcakes

makes 12 jumbo cupcakes

1 recipe White Cake (page 32)	1 recipe Vanilla Bean Frosting (page 37)
1½ cups strawberry jam	
1 recipe Strawberry Frosting	Toppings: edible pearls, edible glitter

1. Prepare White Cake using 2 (6-cup) jumbo muffin pans lined with jumbo paper baking cups coated with cooking spray, filling each cup two-thirds full. Bake for 18 minutes or until a wooden pick inserted in center comes out clean; cool as directed.

2. Fill each cupcake with strawberry jam. (See How-To, page 21.)

3. Frost the top of each cupcake smooth with Strawberry Frosting. (See How-To, page 23.) Insert metal tip no. 3 into a decorating bag; fill with Vanilla Bean Frosting. Write Mom on top of each cupcake. Insert metal tip no. 21 into a decorating bag; fill with Vanilla Bean Frosting. Pipe a border around the top edge of each cupcake. Sprinkle each with edible pearls and edible glitter.

strawberry frosting

½	cup butter, softened	6	cups powdered sugar
½	cup strawberry puree	¼	tsp. salt
1	tsp. strawberry extract (optional)		

1. Beat butter, strawberry puree, and, if desired, extract, at medium speed with an electric mixer until creamy.

2. Gradually add powdered sugar and salt, beating at low speed until blended. Beat at high speed 2 minutes or until creamy. **Makes 3 cups.**

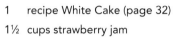

flip it!
Breast Cancer Awareness

• This little cake expresses heartfelt sentiment of another sort when topped with pink sugar ribbons—the emblem for Breast Cancer Awareness. For this flip, use food coloring to tint Vanilla Bean Frosting pink, and frost cupcakes. Rim the cakes with a mix of white sprinkles and tiny pink sugar ribbons. Place 1 large pink sugar ribbon on top of each cupcake.

These little cakes are in honor of man's best friend.

Pup Cakes

makes 48 mini cupcakes

1   recipe Chocolate Cake
1   recipe Chocolate Frosting
     (page 41)

Toppings: chocolate jimmies,
     sugared dog faces

1. Prepare Chocolate Cake using 2 (24-cup) mini muffin pans lined with mini paper baking cups coated with cooking spray, filling each cup two-thirds full. Bake for 10 minutes or until a wooden pick inserted in center comes out clean; cool as directed.

2. Frost each cupcake with Chocolate Frosting using metal tip no. 2D. (See How-To, page 23.) Top each with chocolate jimmies and 1 dog face.

chocolate cake

1   cup Dutch process cocoa
2   cups boiling water
1   cup butter, softened
2   cups superfine sugar
4   large eggs
2¾   cups all-purpose soft-wheat
     flour

1   tsp. baking soda
1   tsp. baking powder
½   tsp. salt
1   tsp. chocolate extract
     Paper baking cups
     Vegetable cooking spray

1. Combine cocoa and 2 cups boiling water in a large heatproof bowl, stirring until blended and smooth; cool completely.

2. Beat butter with a mixer until creamy; gradually add sugar, beating until blended. Add eggs, 1 at a time, beating until blended after each addition.

3. Combine flour and next 3 ingredients; add to butter mixture alternately with cocoa mixture, beginning and ending with flour mixture. Beat at low speed just until blended after each addition. Stir in chocolate extract.

4. Place paper baking cups in 2 (12-cup) muffin pans, and coat with cooking spray; spoon batter into cups, filling two-thirds full.

5. Bake for 12 to 15 minutes. Cool in pans on wire racks 10 minutes; remove from pans, and cool completely. **Makes 24 cupcakes.**

flip it!

Cat Cakes

• For all you cat lovers this is an easy flip—just replace the sugared dog faces with cat faces. Replace chocolate jimmies with orange sprinkles.

baker's secret

• Sugared dog and cat faces are available at cakedeco.com.

Mint Chocolate Chip cupcake has the perfect balance of mint and chocolate. Filled with Chocolate Ganache and covered in creamy Mint Frosting, it smells so inviting.

Mint Chocolate Chip

makes 24 cupcakes

1   recipe Chocolate Cake (page 45)
1   recipe Chocolate Ganache (page 39)
1   recipe Mint Frosting
1   cup crumbled thin crème de menthe chocolate mints

1. Prepare Chocolate Cake as directed.
2. Fill each cupcake with Chocolate Ganache. (See How-To, page 21.)
3. Frost each cupcake with Mint Frosting. (See How-To, page 23.) Top each with crumbled chocolate mints.

Note: We tested with Andes Mints.

mint frosting

½   cup butter, softened
¼   cup whipping cream
1   tsp. peppermint extract
2   drops green liquid food coloring
⅛   tsp. salt
1   (16-oz.) package powdered sugar

1. Beat first 5 ingredients at medium speed with an electric mixer until creamy.
2. Gradually add powdered sugar, beating at low speed until blended. Beat at high speed 2 minutes or until creamy. **Makes 3 cups.**

flip it!

Peppermint Twist

• Flip this recipe with a tasty twist of peppermint. Prepare the Chocolate Cake recipe as directed. Replace the Mint Frosting with Chocolate Ganache. And instead of chocolate mint crumbles, top each cupcake with peppermint candy crumbles.

This cupcake truly tastes like a banana split! You can add all your favorite toppings or just a few.

Banana Split

makes 48 mini cupcakes

1   recipe Banana Cake

1   recipe Vanilla Frosting (page 33)

1   recipe Chocolate Frosting (page 41)

1   recipe Strawberry Frosting (page 42)

Toppings: Chocolate Ganache (page 39), toasted pecans, mini chocolate candies, maraschino cherries

1. Prepare Banana Cake using 2 (24-cup) mini muffin pans lined with mini paper baking cups coated with cooking spray, filling each cup two-thirds full. Bake for 10 minutes or until a wooden pick inserted in center comes out clean; cool as directed.

2. Place 3 mini banana cupcakes in a dessert dish. Place 1 miniature scoop of each flavor of frosting on each cupcake to resemble scoops of ice cream. Top each dessert with a drizzle of Chocolate Ganache, toasted pecans, mini chocolate candies, and 1 cherry.

banana cake

1½ cups mashed ripe bananas

2   tsp. lemon juice

1   cup butter, softened

2   cups sugar

3   large eggs

3   cups all-purpose soft-wheat flour

1½ tsp. baking soda

½   tsp. salt

1½ cups buttermilk

2   tsp. vanilla extract

Paper baking cups

Vegetable cooking spray

1. Preheat oven to 350°.

2. Combine bananas and lemon juice in a small bowl; set aside.

3. Beat butter and sugar at medium speed with an electric mixer until creamy. Add eggs, 1 at a time, beating until blended after each addition.

flip it!

Single-Serving Banana Split

• If you'd rather have your entire banana split in one serving, bake the Banana Cake recipe as directed. Fill each cupcake with Chocolate Ganache, and frost with Vanilla Frosting. Top each with a drizzle of Chocolate Ganache, mini chocolate candies, and 1 cherry.

4. Combine flour, baking soda, and salt. Add to butter mixture alternately with buttermilk, beginning and ending with flour mixture. Beat at low speed just until blended after each addition. Stir in vanilla and reserved banana mixture.

5. Place paper baking cups in 2 (12-cup) muffin pans, and coat with cooking spray; spoon batter into cups, filling two-thirds full.

6. Bake for 12 to 15 minutes or until a wooden pick inserted in center comes out clean. Cool in pans on wire racks 10 minutes; remove from pans to wire racks, and cool completely. **Makes 24 cupcakes.**

One of our most requested flavors, this cupcake is a combination of salty and sweet blended with mocha.

Caramel-Mocha-Sea Salt

makes 24 cupcakes

1   recipe Chocolate Cake (page 45)

1   recipe Mocha Frosting

Toppings: Caramel Drizzle, coarse sea salt, candy espresso beans

1. Prepare Chocolate Cake as directed.

2. Frost each cupcake with Mocha Frosting using metal tip no. 12. (See How-To, page 23.) Drizzle each cupcake with Caramel Drizzle; top each with about ⅛ tsp. sea salt and 1 espresso bean.

mocha frosting

1   cup butter, softened
¾   cup unsweetened cocoa
¼   tsp. salt
2   tsp. coffee extract

2   (16-oz.) packages powdered sugar
⅓   cup whipping cream

1. Beat first 4 ingredients at medium speed with an electric mixer until creamy.

2. Gradually add powdered sugar alternately with cream, beating at low speed until blended after each addition. Beat at high speed 2 minutes or until creamy. **Makes about 5 cups.**

caramel drizzle

½   cup butter
1   cup sugar

1   cup whipping cream

1. Cook butter and sugar in a 2-qt. heavy saucepan over high heat, stirring occasionally, until mixture is caramel-colored, about 4 to 5 minutes. Remove from heat, and slowly add cream, stirring constantly until blended.

2. Return to heat, and bring to a boil; cook 1 to 2 minutes, stirring occasionally. Cool. **Makes about 1½ cups.**

baker's secret

• If you're dying to try this recipe but don't have coffee extract in your pantry, you can dissolve 2 Tbsp. instant espresso in ¼ cup hot water as a substitution.

flip it!

Love in Bloom

• Replace Poppy Seed Cake with Lemon–Poppy Seed Cake (see baker's secret, below), and frost with Wedding Cake Frosting that's been tinted red. Top with pink bubble sprinkles and a sugared flower, and you'll have a sweet little cake that's perfect for any special occasion. To tint the frosting, stir red liquid food coloring into Wedding Cake Frosting until frosting reaches the desired tint.

baker's secret

• For Lemon–Poppy Seed Cake, substitute lemon extract for vanilla, and add 2 to 3 Tbsp. finely grated lemon zest to batter when stirring in extract and poppy seeds.

I've been making these cupcakes since my kids were little. Now we make them for every birthday and holiday they celebrate. We call this recipe Paparazzi because it has star quality.

Paparazzi

makes 24 cupcakes

1	recipe Poppy Seed Cake	Multicolored sparkling sugar
1	recipe Wedding Cake Frosting (page 31)	

1. Prepare Poppy Seed Cake as directed.

2. Frost each cupcake with Wedding Cake Frosting using metal tip no. 21. (See How-To, page 23.) Top each with sparkling sugar.

poppy seed cake

1	cup butter, softened	¼	tsp. salt
2⅓	cups sugar	1	cup sour cream
5	large eggs	1	tsp. vanilla extract
3	cups all-purpose soft-wheat flour	2	Tbsp. poppy seeds
¼	tsp. baking soda		Paper baking cups
			Vegetable cooking spray

1. Preheat oven to 350°.

2. Beat butter at medium speed with an electric mixer until creamy; gradually add sugar, beating well. Add eggs, 1 at a time, beating until blended after each addition.

3. Combine flour, baking soda, and salt; add to butter mixture alternately with sour cream, beginning and ending with flour mixture. Beat at low speed until blended after each addition. Stir in vanilla and poppy seeds.

4. Place paper baking cups in 2 (12-cup) muffin pans, and coat with cooking spray; spoon batter into cups, filling two-thirds full.

5. Bake for 12 to 15 minutes or until a wooden pick inserted in center comes out clean. Cool in pans on wire racks 10 minutes; remove from pans to wire racks, and cool completely. **Makes 24 cupcakes.**

Cookies and Cream cupcakes are irresistible! The creamy vanilla frosting is jam-packed with crushed cookies. A tall glass of milk is all you need to complete this luscious treat.

Cookies and Cream

makes 24 cupcakes

1	recipe Chocolate Cake (page 45)	24	cream-filled miniature chocolate sandwich cookies (whole or coarsely crushed)
2	recipes Cookies and Cream Frosting		

1. Prepare Chocolate Cake as directed.
2. Fill each cupcake with Cookies and Cream Frosting. (See How-to, page 21.)
3. Frost each cupcake with Cookies and Cream Frosting using metal tip no. 12. (See How-To, page 23.) Top each with 1 sandwich cookie or, if desired, crushed cookie pieces.

cookies and cream frosting

½	cup butter, softened	2	tsp. clear vanilla extract
1	(16-oz.) package powdered sugar	15	cream-filled miniature chocolate sandwich cookies, finely crushed
⅓	cup whipping cream		
⅛	tsp. salt		

1. Beat butter at medium speed with an electric mixer until creamy.
2. Gradually add powdered sugar, alternately with cream, beating at low speed until blended. Add salt and vanilla, beating until blended. Stir in crushed cookies until combined. Beat at high speed 2 minutes or until creamy. Makes 4 cups.

These sunny cupcakes are definitely for lemon lovers. The rich, moist, lemony cupcakes are filled with lemon and topped with lots of frosting. We love the little lemon candy slice on top, but a fresh one is even better. If you can find Meyer lemons, they are the best!

Lemon Love

makes 24 cupcakes

1   recipe Lemon Cake
1   drop yellow liquid food coloring

1   recipe Lemon Frosting
Candy lemon slices

1. Prepare Lemon Cake as directed.
2. Fill each cupcake with Lemon Frosting. (See How-To, page 21.)
3. Frost each cupcake with Lemon Frosting. (See How-To, page 23.) Top each with 1 candy lemon slice.

lemon cake

¾   cup milk
¼   cup fresh lemon juice (about 2 lemons)
½   tsp. lemon oil or lemon extract
Zest of 1 lemon (optional)
1   cup butter, softened
2   cups sugar

4   large eggs
3   cups all-purpose soft-wheat flour
2   tsp. baking powder
1   tsp. salt
Paper baking cups
Cooking spray

1. Preheat oven to 350°.
2. Combine milk, lemon juice, lemon oil, and, if desired, zest in a small bowl; set aside.
3. Beat butter and sugar at medium speed with an electric mixer until creamy. Add eggs, 1 at a time, beating until blended after each addition.
4. Combine flour, baking powder, and salt. Add to butter mixture alternately with milk mixture, beginning and ending with flour mixture. Beat at low speed just until blended after each addition.

5. Place paper baking cups in 2 (12-cup) muffin pans, and coat with cooking spray; spoon batter into cups, filling two-thirds full.

6. Bake for 12 to 15 minutes or until a wooden pick inserted in center comes out clean. Cool in pans on wire racks 10 minutes; remove from pans to wire racks, and cool completely. **Makes 24 cupcakes.**

lemon frosting

1	cup butter, softened	1	tsp. lemon zest (optional)
⅛	tsp. salt	2	(16-oz.) packages powdered
3	Tbsp. fresh lemon juice		sugar
1	tsp. lemon oil or lemon extract	¼	cup whipping cream
2	to 4 drops yellow liquid food coloring		

1. Beat first 5 ingredients and, if desired, zest at medium speed with an electric mixer until creamy.

2. Gradually add powdered sugar alternately with cream, beating at low speed until blended after each addition. Beat at high speed 2 minutes or until creamy. **Makes 6 cups.**

For those who find it hard to make up their minds about what flavor they want, we have our Neapolitan. Besides being beautiful to look at, it has the best of everything. Strawberry Cake, a chocolate filling, and vanilla, chocolate, and strawberry frostings. It is simple, yet elegant, even for a cupcake.

Neapolitan

makes 24 cupcakes

1	recipe Strawberry Cake (page 34)	1	recipe Vanilla Frosting (page 33)
2	recipes Chocolate Frosting (page 41)	1	recipe Strawberry Frosting (page 42)

1. Prepare Strawberry Cake as directed.

2. Fill each cupcake with Chocolate Frosting. (See How-To, page 21.)

3. Frost the top of each cupcake smooth with Vanilla Frosting. (See How-To, page 23.) Insert metal tip no. 2D into a decorating bag; fill with Strawberry Frosting, and pipe a border on one half of each cupcake. Insert metal tip no. 2D into a decorating bag; fill with Chocolate Frosting, and pipe a border on the other half of each cupcake to form a circle of frosting.

flip it!

Black 'n' White

• Flip the tri-flavored Neapolitan recipe into a classic, two-tone, two-flavor treat. Replace the Strawberry Cake with White Cake (page 32) or Chocolate Cake (page 45), and omit the Strawberry Frosting.

Mississippi Mud is one of my most favorite recipes from childhood. We always made it in a large sheet pan, covered the top with marshmallows while it was hot from the oven, sprinkled on a handful of toasted pecans, and then poured the chocolate fudge frosting over it. We could never wait for it to cool. The warm gooey marshmallows and chocolate in cupcake form is just as delicious.

Mississippi Mud

makes 12 jumbo cupcakes

1 recipe Chocolate Cake (page 45)	1½ cups miniature marshmallows
	1 recipe Fudge Frosting

1. Prepare Chocolate Cake using 2 (6-cup) jumbo muffin pans lined with jumbo paper baking cups coated with cooking spray, filling each cup about half full. Bake for 15 minutes or until a wooden pick inserted in center comes out clean. Do not cool.

2. Top each cupcake while still hot with 2 Tbsp. miniature marshmallows.

3. Pour Fudge Frosting over the top of each cupcake, almost covering marshmallows.

fudge frosting

½	cup butter	4	cups powdered sugar
⅓	cup evaporated milk	½	tsp. vanilla extract
¼	cup unsweetened cocoa	¼	tsp. salt

1. Combine first 3 ingredients in a small saucepan; cook over medium heat until butter melts and mixture is blended. Bring mixture to a boil, stirring constantly. Remove from heat; add powdered sugar, vanilla, and salt, whisking until smooth. Pour immediately over cupcakes. Makes 4 cups.

flip it!

Rocky Road

• Turn Mississippi Mud into a classic Rocky Road. Pour the Fudge Frosting over each cupcake, and then top with toasted, chopped pecans and miniature marshmallows.

We're always looking for ways to turn our favorite desserts into cupcake form. Lemon Ice Box is one that we all agree hits the mark. We like these extra tart and lemony. If you prefer not to use whipped cream, Vanilla Frosting tastes just as wonderful.

Lemon Ice Box

makes 24 cupcakes

1   recipe White Cake (page 32)
1   recipe Lemon Ice Box Filling
1   recipe Fresh Whipped Cream

Toppings: graham cracker crumbs, candy lemon slices (cut in half), fresh lemon slices (optional)

1. Prepare White Cake as directed.

2. Fill each cupcake with Lemon Ice Box Filling. (See How-To, page 21.)

3. Frost each cupcake with Fresh Whipped Cream. (See How-To, page 23.) Sprinkle each with graham cracker crumbs, and top each with 2 candy lemon wedges or, if desired, 1 fresh lemon slice.

lemon ice box filling

1   (14-oz.) can sweetened condensed milk

½   cup fresh lemon juice (about 3 lemons)
1   tsp. lemon zest

1. Combine all ingredients in a small bowl, stirring until well blended. Cover and chill until thick. Makes 2 cups.

Note: Store any remaining filling in refrigerator up to 1 week.

fresh whipped cream

1½   cup whipping cream, chilled
2   tsp. vanilla extract

¼   cup sugar

1. Beat whipping cream at high speed with an electric mixer until soft peaks form. Add vanilla and sugar, and beat until stiff peaks form. Store in refrigerator until ready to use. Makes 3 cups.

flip it!

Daisy Chain

• Frost Lemon Ice Box cupcakes with Lemon Frosting (page 57) instead of Fresh Whipped Cream for a fresh-as-springtime taste. Add a cute daisy pick to carry out the seasonal theme.

Dreamcakes can never make enough of our Banana Pudding cupcakes. They are the ultimate comfort food. The creamy Fresh Banana Curd is a treat all its own, but pair it with our Banana Cake and whipped cream, and you'll come running back for more.

Banana Pudding

makes 24 cupcakes

flip it!

Banana Cream Pie

• Flip this banana-flavored favorite from a pudding to a pie. Use metal tip no. 2D to pipe Fresh Whipped Cream onto each cupcake. Swap the vanilla wafers for a sprinkling of graham cracker crumbs.

1   recipe Banana Cake (page 48)
1   recipe Fresh Banana Curd
3   cups Fresh Whipped Cream (page 63)

Toppings: vanilla wafers and fresh banana slices

1. Prepare Banana Cake as directed.

2. Fill each cupcake with Fresh Banana Curd. (See How-To, page 21.)

3. Pipe 2 Tbsp. Fresh Whipped Cream onto each cupcake using metal tip no. 12. Top with 1 vanilla wafer and 1 banana slice just before serving.

fresh banana curd

4   large ripe bananas, peeled
4   Tbsp. butter
1½   cups sugar
2   Tbsp. fresh lemon juice
4   large eggs

1. Mash bananas in a large bowl with a fork until creamy.

2. Combine mashed banana and remaining ingredients in a medium saucepan over medium-low heat. Cook, whisking constantly, until mixture thickens and coats a spoon. (Do not boil.) Cool completely. Makes 2 cups.

Note: Store any leftover curd in an airtight container in refrigerator for up to 3 days.

Old-Fashioned Caramel is a cupcake that can't be rushed. It's a true labor of love. The caramel has to cool for a while before you can make the frosting, and then you need to use the frosting right away. If the frosting gets too thick to spread, add just a little cream or milk to make it spreadable. It is definitely worth the effort.

Old-Fashioned Caramel

makes 24 cupcakes

1 recipe Butter Cake (page 40)

1 recipe Old-Fashioned Caramel Frosting

1. Prepare Butter Cake as directed.

2. Frost each cupcake with Old-Fashioned Caramel Frosting. (See How-To, page 23.)

old-fashioned caramel frosting

1 cup butter

1 (16-oz.) package dark brown sugar

½ cup evaporated milk

¼ tsp. baking soda

1 Tbsp. light corn syrup

4 cups powdered sugar

1. Melt butter in a 3-qt. heavy saucepan over medium heat. Add brown sugar; bring to a boil, stirring constantly. Stir in evaporated milk, baking soda, and corn syrup; bring to a boil. Remove from heat, and let cool completely (about 1 hour). Transfer to a bowl.

2. Gradually add powdered sugar to caramel mixture, beating at medium speed with an electric mixer until blended. Beat at high speed 2 minutes or until creamy. Use immediately. **Makes 3 cups.**

baker's secret

• Baking soda helps to prevent the caramel from becoming grainy.

Our Little Carrot Cakes are a tribute to Beatrix Potter's character Peter Rabbit. He loved carrots, so we loaded a "bunch" into these.

Little Carrot Cakes

makes 48 mini cupcakes

3	large eggs	2½	cups finely grated carrot
1	cup granulated sugar	1	cup crushed pineapple, drained
1	cup firmly packed dark brown sugar	2	cups sweetened flaked coconut
¾	cup canola oil	2	cups toasted chopped pecans
¾	cup buttermilk		Mini paper baking cups
2	cups all-purpose soft-wheat flour		Vegetable cooking spray
2	tsp. baking soda	1	recipe Glaze
½	tsp. salt	1	recipe Cream Cheese Frosting (page 35)
1½	tsp. ground cinnamon		Toppings: orange sprinkles and sugar carrots
2	tsp. vanilla extract		

1. Preheat oven to 350°.

2. Beat eggs and next 4 ingredients in a large bowl at medium speed with an electric mixer until creamy.

3. Combine flour and next 3 ingredients; add to egg mixture, beating at low speed until blended. Stir in vanilla and next 4 ingredients.

4. Place paper baking cups in 2 (24-cup) mini muffin pans, and coat with cooking spray; spoon batter into cups, filling two-thirds full.

5. Bake for 10 minutes or until a wooden pick inserted in center comes out clean. Cool slightly in pans. Brush glaze evenly over warm cupcakes. Cool in pans on wire racks 10 minutes; remove from pans to wire racks, and cool completely. Frost each cupcake with Cream Cheese Frosting using metal tip no. 2D. (See How-To, page 23.) Top each with orange sprinkles and 1 candy carrot.

baker's secret

• Brushing the warm glaze over the cupcakes makes a moist, dense, delicious cake.

• Sugar carrots can be found at cakedeco.com.

glaze

¾ cup sugar

½ cup buttermilk

½ cup butter

1. Bring all ingredients to a boil in a 2-qt. heavy saucepan over medium-high heat. Cook, stirring often, 5 minutes. Remove from heat. Cool slightly, about 15 minutes. **Makes 1½ cups.**

Anyone who knows me knows my obsession with birds, eggs, and nests. The tiny little chocolate nests that top these cupcakes give me so much joy to make. I like Jelly Belly's Ice Cream Shop blend of jelly beans; they look the most like tiny little eggs just waiting to hatch.

Spring Bird's Nest

makes 24 cupcakes

1	recipe Poppy Seed Cake (page 52)		Teal food coloring gel
2	recipes Vanilla Frosting (page 33)		Chocolate Birds' Nests
		24	candy pansies (optional)

1. Prepare Poppy Seed Cake as directed.
2. Tint Vanilla Frosting using teal food coloring gel.
3. Fill each cupcake with tinted frosting. (See How-To, page 21.)
4. Frost each cupcake with tinted frosting. (See How-To, page 23.)
5. Top each cupcake with 1 bird's nest and, if desired, 1 candy pansy.

chocolate birds' nests

4	(1-oz.) squares chocolate almond bark candy coating, melted	1	(5-oz.) can crispy rice noodles
			Jelly beans (about 1 cup)

1. In a medium bowl, combine melted candy coating and rice noodles until noodles are completely coated.
2. Spoon 2 to 3 Tbsp. chocolate mixture into each cup of a lightly greased miniature muffin pan. Make an indentation in center of each to form a bird's nest. Chill 10 minutes or until chocolate is set. Pop nests from muffin pan, and place 2 to 3 jelly beans in each nest. Makes 24 nests.

Note: We tested with La Choy for the rice noodles.

flip it!

Easter Parade

• You can turn our little bird's nest cakes into cute baskets just perfect for Easter. Tint the Vanilla Frosting a dark teal color with food coloring gel. Omit the Chocolate Birds' Nests, and wrap each cupcake in a basket cupcake liner. Top each cupcake with chocolate candy eggs (such as Cadbury mini eggs) and pastel-colored sprinkles.

baker's secret

• Nests can be made ahead and stored up to 2 weeks in an airtight container until ready to use.
• Basket cupcake liners for Easter Parade are available at wilton.com.

Many of our cupcakes are inspired by art, people, or literature. "Starry Night" by Vincent van Gogh inspired this swirling confection of frostings tinted to mimic that painting. We top these off with edible glitter stars that can be found online at cakedeco.com.

Starry Night

makes 24 cupcakes

1	recipe Marble Cake	Food coloring gel in purple, green,
2	recipes Vanilla Bean Frosting	blue, and yellow
	(page 37)	Edible glitter stars

1. Prepare Marble Cake as directed.

2. To prepare frosting, place about 1 cup Vanilla Bean Frosting in each of 4 small bowls. Using food coloring gels, tint frosting in each of 4 bowls a different color.

3. Stir colored frostings together until gently marbled. Frost each cupcake with marbled frosting using metal tip no. 2D. (See How-To, page 23.) Top with edible glitter stars.

marble cake

½	recipe Chocolate Cake	Paper baking cups
	(page 45)	Vegetable cooking spray
½	recipe White Cake (page 32)	

1. Prepare half recipes of Chocolate Cake batter and White Cake batter.

2. Place paper baking cups in 2 (12-cup) muffin pans, and coat with cooking spray; spoon 3 Tbsp. of each batter in each cup. Using a knife, stir batters gently until marbled.

3. Bake for 15 minutes or until a wooden pick inserted in center comes out clean. Cool in pans on wire racks 10 minutes; remove from pans to wire racks, and cool completely. Makes 24 cupcakes.

flip it!

Monet Cupcakes

• Create a Monet masterpiece by substituting bright pastel-colored frostings for van Gogh's rich dark blues and greens. Omit the edible glitter stars.

Chai is an intensely flavorful spiced black tea combined with milk. It's very good for you but can be time consuming to make. Using chai concentrate makes this recipe a cinch and gives a really rich flavor to the cake and frosting. This is our version of a chai latte in cupcake form.

Chai Cupcakes

makes 24 cupcakes

1   recipe Chai Cake
2   recipes Chai–Cream Cheese Frosting
Ground cinnamon

½   cup Chai–Cream Cheese Frosting
Brown food coloring gel

1. Prepare Chai Cake as directed.
2. Fill each cupcake with Chai–Cream Cheese Frosting. (See How-To, page 21.)
3. Frost each cupcake with Chai–Cream Cheese Frosting. (See How-To, page 23.) Sprinkle each with cinnamon.
4. Tint ½ cup Chai–Cream Cheese Frosting with brown gel food coloring. Insert metal tip no. 3 into a decorating bag, and fill with frosting. Pipe oriental symbols on top of each cupcake.

chai cake

½   cup butter, softened
1   cup shortening
2   cups sugar
4   large eggs
¾   cup milk
¼   cup chai tea concentrate

2¾ cups all-purpose soft-wheat flour
2   tsp. baking powder
½   tsp. salt
Paper baking cups
Vegetable cooking spray

1. Preheat oven to 350°.
2. Beat butter and shortening at medium speed with an electric mixer until creamy; gradually add sugar, beating well. Add eggs, 1 at a time, beating until blended after each addition.

3. Combine milk and chai concentrate in a small bowl.

4. Combine flour, baking powder, and salt; add to butter mixture alternately with milk mixture, beginning and ending with flour mixture. Beat at low speed until blended after each addition.

5. Place paper baking cups in 2 (12-cup) muffin pans, and coat with cooking spray; spoon batter into cups, filling two-thirds full.

6. Bake for 12 to 15 minutes or until a wooden pick inserted in center comes out clean. Cool in pans on wire racks 10 minutes; remove from pans to wire racks, and cool completely. Makes 24 cupcakes.

Note: We tested with Oregon Chai's Chai Tea Latte Concentrate.

chai–cream cheese frosting

½	cup butter, softened	3	Tbsp. chai tea concentrate
1	(8-oz.) package cream cheese, softened	4	cups powdered sugar
		¼	tsp. salt

1. Beat butter, cream cheese, and chai concentrate at medium speed with an electric mixer until creamy.

2. Gradually add powdered sugar and salt, beating at low speed until blended. Beat at high speed 2 minutes or until creamy. Makes 3 cups.

Summer Celebrations

Refreshing lemons and limes, juicy blackberries and peaches, and a fragrant blend of all our favorite summertime flavors fill our bakery cases. So grab your flip flops and sunglasses, and kick up your feet with a celebration of summer—Dreamcakes-style.

During the summer, we take advantage of the abundance of fresh blueberries. By visiting several local farms, we are able to pick blueberries by the bucketful. We like to make our own blueberry preserves, because it is so simple to do and we use it so quickly. We stir a little of the preserves into this batter, because we love the beautiful blue color you find when you bite into the cupcake.

Big Blue

makes 24 cupcakes

3	cups all-purpose soft-wheat flour	2	cups blueberry preserves, divided
1½	cups sugar	2	cups fresh blueberries
4	tsp. baking powder		Paper baking cups
½	tsp. salt		Vegetable cooking spray
¾	cup milk	3	cups Fresh Whipped Cream (page 63)
⅔	cup vegetable oil		Fresh sugared blueberries
2	large eggs		

1. Preheat oven to 350°.

2. Combine first 4 ingredients in a large bowl; make a well in center of mixture.

3. Stir together milk, oil, eggs, and ½ cup blueberry preserves; add to dry mixture, stirring just until moistened. Fold in blueberries.

4. Place paper baking cups in 2 (12-cup) muffin pans, and coat with cooking spray; spoon batter into cups, filling two-thirds full.

5. Bake for 12 to 15 minutes or until a wooden pick inserted in center comes out clean. Cool in pans on wire racks 10 minutes; remove from pans to wire racks, and cool completely.

6. Fill cupcakes with 1 Tbsp. each of remaining blueberry preserves. (See How-To, page 21.) Pipe 2 Tbsp. Fresh Whipped Cream onto each cupcake using metal tip no. 12. (See How-To, page 23.) Top each with sugared blueberries.

Blackberries flourish all summer long in the South. They grow anywhere and everywhere and are free for the picking. They have prickly thorns, but if you're careful, you can have a bucketful of plump, juicy berries in no time. The only cost may be a few scratches and purple fingers, but you'll have gained lots of berries to share—if you're feeling generous. When you toss the sugar with the berries, they begin to release their sweet juice, so don't put the berries on the cupcakes until just before serving. We love when the juice trickles down the sides and makes a puddle on the plate; you may want to eat this one with a spoon.

Blackberry Summer

makes 24 cupcakes

1 recipe Butter Cake (page 40)	1 pt. fresh blackberries
1¾ cups seedless blackberry jam, divided	3 Tbsp. sugar
1 recipe Vanilla Frosting (page 33)	

1. Prepare Butter Cake as directed.

2. Fill each cupcake using 1½ cups blackberry jam. (See How-To, page 21.)

3. Stir remaining ¼ cup jam into Vanilla Frosting. Frost each cupcake with flavored frosting. (See How-To, page 23.)

4. Toss together blackberries and sugar. Top each cupcake with blackberries just before serving.

If you are looking for a chocolate fix, look no further. This is layer upon layer of chocolate. Moist Chocolate Cake, a mountain of Chocolate Frosting, and a sprinkle of chocolate chunks. If you feel the need for a little more, fill the cupcakes with Chocolate Ganache. This one is guaranteed to fulfill any chocolate lover's dream.

Chocolate-Chocolate Chunk

makes 24 cupcakes

1 recipe Chocolate Cake (page 45)

1 recipe Chocolate Frosting (page 41)

1½ cups chocolate chunks

1. Prepare Chocolate Cake as directed.

2. Frost each cupcake with Chocolate Frosting using metal tip no. 2D. (See How-To, page 23.) Top each with about 1 Tbsp. chocolate chunks.

flip it!

White Chocolate Chunk

• For a "lighter" version, prepare White Cake (page 32), and frost each cupcake with Vanilla Bean Frosting (page 37); top each with white chocolate chunks.

I can never decide if my favorite part of a Creamsicle is the tart orange outside or the creamy vanilla inside. One thing is for sure: It's a classic summer pairing. For fun, we serve our version with a big, bright orange gumball and an old-fashioned wooden ice cream spoon, just like the ice cream man. No worries about this one melting, but you still may want to lick your fingers.

Orange Cream Dream

makes 24 cupcakes

1   recipe White Cake (page 32)
1   recipe Classic Orange Frosting
1   to 2 drops orange liquid food
     coloring

Toppings: white sprinkles, orange
     gumballs
Garnish: wooden ice cream spoons

1. Prepare White Cake as directed.

2. Tint Classic Orange Frosting with food coloring. Frost each cupcake with tinted frosting. (See How-To, page 23.) Top each with sprinkles and 1 orange gumball; garnish each with 1 wooden ice cream spoon.

classic orange frosting

½   cup butter, softened
¼   cup whipping cream
1   tsp. orange flavoring

⅛   tsp. salt
1   (16-oz.) package powdered
     sugar

1. Beat first 4 ingredients at medium speed with an electric mixer until creamy.

2. Gradually add powdered sugar, beating at low speed until blended. Beat at high speed 2 minutes or until creamy. Makes 3 cups.

flip it!
Orange Blossom Cupcakes

• For a more intense flavor experience, tint Classic Orange Frosting a darker orange, and top each cupcake with candy orange slices.

baker's secret

• LorAnn Gourmet makes a wonderful line of flavored extracts, oils, and emulsions for baking. They give a burst of flavor to your cakes and frostings. A little goes a long way, so be careful and don't overdo it. We especially love the Orange Bakery Emulsion.

Dean Martin, the "King of Cool," is a classic, and so is our That's Amore marble cupcake. Just the right mix of chocolate and vanilla with a glamorous gold topping.

That's Amore

makes 24 cupcakes

1	recipe Marble Cake (page 72)	Toppings: edible gold dragées,
½	recipe Vanilla Frosting (page 33)	gold sparkling sugar
½	recipe Chocolate Frosting (page 41)	

1. Prepare Marble Cake as directed.

2. Insert metal tip no. 2D into a decorating bag; fill with ½ cup Vanilla Frosting and ½ cup Chocolate Frosting. Pipe a generous peak of marbled frosting on each cupcake. Refill decorating bag with frosting as needed. Top each with gold dragées and sanding sugar, if desired.

Our Mocha Latte cupcake is a double shot of flavor. Espresso powder gives a deep, rich flavor to the chocolate cake. We spread on a thick layer of Vanilla Frosting, drizzle it with caramel and chocolate, and top it off with sprinkles—and you don't have to wait in the drive-thru for it.

Mocha Latte

makes 24 cupcakes

1   recipe Mocha Cake

1   recipe Vanilla Frosting
     (page 33)

Toppings: Caramel Drizzle (page 51),
     Chocolate Ganache (page 39),
     chocolate jimmies

1. Prepare Mocha Cake as directed.

2. Frost each cupcake with Vanilla Frosting using metal tip no. 12. (See How-To, page 23.) Drizzle each cupcake with caramel and chocolate, and top each with chocolate jimmies.

mocha cake

2   cups boiling water

1   cup Dutch process cocoa

1   to 2 Tbsp. instant espresso

1   cup butter, softened

2   cups fine granulated sugar or
     castor sugar

4   large eggs

2¾   cups all-purpose soft-wheat
     flour

1   tsp. baking soda

1   tsp. baking powder

½   tsp. salt

1   tsp. chocolate extract or
     vanilla extract

Paper baking cups

Vegetable cooking spray

1. Stir together boiling water, cocoa, and espresso until smooth; let cool.

2. Beat butter at medium speed with an electric mixer until creamy; gradually add sugar, beating well. Add eggs, 1 at a time, beating until blended after each addition.

3. Combine flour and next 3 ingredients; add to butter mixture alternately with cocoa mixture, beginning and ending with flour mixture. Beat

at low speed until blended after each addition. Stir in chocolate extract.

4. Place paper baking cups in 2 (12-cup) muffin pans, and coat with cooking spray; spoon batter into cups, filling two-thirds full.

5. Bake for 12 to 15 minutes or until a wooden pick inserted in center comes out clean. Cool in pans on wire racks 10 minutes; remove from pans to wire racks, and cool completely. Makes 24 cupcakes.

These light little bites are the most adorable sweet treats for an afternoon tea. Edible flowers were especially popular during Queen Victoria's reign; we think she would be pleased with this addition to tea time. Be sure your blossoms are nonpoisonous and free of pesticides. We've listed a few below that we think are lovely for any garden party.

flip it!
Earth Day

• Earth Day cupcake is intended to inspire awareness and appreciation for the Earth's natural environment. Omit the edible flowers. Tint our Vanilla Frosting (page 33) in shades of deep blue and green. Frost the tops of each cupcake smooth with the blue frosting. Using metal tip no. 4, pipe each with designs in green frosting to look like our lovely green planet.

Garden Party

makes 48 mini cupcakes

1   recipe Angel Food Cake
    (page 124)
1   recipe Mascarpone Frosting
    (page 145)

Edible flower blossoms

1. Prepare Angel Food Cake using 2 (24-cup) mini muffin pans lined with mini paper baking cups coated with cooking spray, filling each cup two-thirds full. Bake for 10 minutes or until a wooden pick inserted in center comes out clean; cool as directed.

2. Insert metal tip no. 21 into a large decorating bag; fill with frosting. Pipe a small circle of frosting in the center of each cupcake. Top each with an edible flower blossom. You may prefer to remove the flower before eating the cupcake.

baker's secret

• Some edible blossoms we like are pansies, lavender, violets, and roses. Be sure to research any flowers you want to eat. You must be certain they are edible and that they have been grown organically (without the use of pesticides). North Carolina State University has a fantastic web site with an extensive nonpoisonous and poisonous listing. Check it out at www.ces.ncsu.edu/depts/hort/hil/hil-8513.html. You can also visit the Colorado State University Extension's web site at www.ext.colostate.edu/pubs/garden/07237.html for tips on picking the flowers and using them.

For those who are more about the icing than the cake, our Icing Shots are just the ticket. A small tumbler of your favorite icing is sometimes all you need to bring a little happiness to your day.

Icing Shots

makes 24 servings

½ recipe Chocolate Frosting (page 41)

½ recipe Mint Frosting (page 46)

½ recipe Strawberry Frosting (page 42)

½ recipe Vanilla Bean Frosting (page 37), tinted blue

Candy sticks (optional)

1. Prepare your favorite frosting. (We've listed some favorites above.)

2. Pipe frosting into small tumblers or cups using metal tip no. 2D. (See How-To, page 23.)

3. Use flavored candy sticks to enjoy this treat.

The creamy Key Lime Filling tastes like sunshine captured in a cupcake. Key limes are easy to find these days. They are small, golf ball–sized limes with a pale yellow and green color. If you can't find them, bottled Key lime juice works well.

Key Lime Cupcakes

makes 24 cupcakes

1 recipe White Cake (page 32)

1 recipe Key Lime Filling

3 cups Fresh Whipped Cream (page 63)

Toppings: graham cracker crumbs, lime rind strips

1. Prepare White Cake as directed.

2. Fill each cupcake with Key Lime Filling. (See How-To, page 21.)

3. Frost each cupcake with Fresh Whipped Cream. (See How-To, page 23.) Top with graham cracker crumbs and lime rind.

key lime filling

1 (14-ounce) can sweetened condensed milk

⅓ cup Key lime juice

1 Tbsp. lime zest

1. Stir together all ingredients in a medium bowl until blended. Chill 1 hour or until thick. Makes 2 cups.

One great advantage of summer is the abundance of fresh basil. Pair it with fresh lemon, and you get a flavor duo that few can rival. We simply dust these cupcakes with powdered sugar so the full flavors come through. It's just right for those hot summer days when you want something light and not too sweet.

Lemon-Basil

makes 24 cupcakes

1 recipe Lemon Cake (page 56)	¼ cup fresh basil leaves, cut into thin strips
3 Tbsp. powdered sugar	
¼ cup lemon rind curls	

1. Prepare Lemon Cake as directed.

2. Dust each cooled cupcake with powdered sugar. Top each with ½ tsp. lemon rind curls and ½ tsp. fresh basil.

Note: Prepare lemon and basil topping just before serving.

Lemon-Coconut is a tropical delight filled with a tart raspberry filling. We use fresh shards of coconut for an impressive presentation, but any coconut will do.

Lemon-Coconut

makes 24 cupcakes

1   recipe Lemon Cake (page 56)
1½ cups seedless raspberry jam
1   recipe Lemon Frosting
      (page 57)

Toppings: fresh coconut shards,
      fresh raspberries

1. Prepare Lemon Cake as directed.
2. Fill each cupcake with raspberry jam. (See How-To, page 21.)
3. Frost each cupcake with Lemon Frosting. (See How-To, page 23.) Top each with coconut, and serve with fresh raspberries.

Enchanting bites of moist lemon cake, a zing of crystallized ginger, and the tang of fresh lemon zest make for an unexpected, sweet "amuse-bouche" (similar to an hors d'oeuvre) for your cocktail party. We love these with champagne. I actually love anything with champagne.

Lemon-Ginger

makes 48 mini cupcakes

1 recipe Lemon Cake (page 56)
1 recipe Lemon Frosting (page 57)

Toppings: finely chopped crystallized ginger, lemon rind curls

1. Prepare Lemon Cake using 2 (24-cup) mini muffin pans lined with mini paper baking cups coated with cooking spray, filling each cup two-thirds full. Bake for 10 minutes or until a wooden pick inserted in center comes out clean; cool as directed.

2. Insert metal tip no. 12 into a decorating bag; fill with Lemon Frosting. Pipe a small cap of frosting on each cupcake. Top each with crystallized ginger and lemon rind curls.

flip it!
Lady Bug

• Frost each cupcake with green frosting, pulling upward to look like grass. Using metal tip no. 3 and red frosting, pipe ladybugs onto cupcakes. Using black frosting, pipe a head, antennae, and dots. Top with yellow sprinkles.

baker's secret

• Cute little candy mushrooms can be purchased seasonally at auiswiss.com. We usually have a good supply of these mushrooms at the bakery and can sell them if we have enough in stock. Visit our web site at dreamcakes-bakery.com for more information including our email address and phone number.

My mother once told me a story when I was about 5 years old, that if you were lucky, you could sometimes catch a glimpse of fairies dancing under the little circle of mushrooms growing in the grass. One day I spent a whole afternoon watching for fairies. You may not see fairies under our cupcakes, but they are very merry!

Merry Cherry Mushrooms

makes 24 assorted cupcakes

1 recipe White Cake (page 32)	White rolled fondant
1 recipe Wedding Cake Frosting (page 31)	Paper baking cups in assorted sizes
3 Tbsp. maraschino cherry juice	Red and green food coloring gel
	Candy mushrooms

1. Prepare White Cake as directed, dividing batter into 4 jumbo-size muffin cups, 8 regular-size muffin cups, and 12 mini muffin cups. Cool as directed.

2. Stir together Wedding Cake Frosting and cherry juice. Divide frosting into 2 medium bowls. Tint 1 bowl of frosting with desired amount of red food coloring gel and 1 bowl of frosting with desired amount of green food coloring gel. Frost 4 regular and 4 mini-size cupcakes smooth with green frosting. Frost all remaining cupcakes smooth with red frosting.

3. Roll fondant out to ⅛-inch thickness. Using the larger end of metal tips no. 12 and no. 2D (not the piping end), cut out circles from the white fondant. Place 5 to 6 white polka dots on all red frosted cupcakes while frosting is still wet (so fondant will adhere).

4. Place 1 mini red mushroom cupcake on top of 1 regular green frosted cupcake, if desired. Secure with a wooden pick, if necessary. Place 2 to 3 small candy mushrooms on the mini green cupcakes.

5. Arrange all cupcakes on a platter mixing the sizes and colors together for a merry cherry festive display.

Nothing could be better on a sultry summer evening than an ice cold mojito. The splendid blend of mint, lime, and rum is so refreshing. It's the inspiration for Dreamcakes' Mojito Cupcakes. Go ahead and stir up a batch; it's 5 o'clock somewhere.

Mojito Cupcakes

makes 24 cupcakes

1 recipe White Cake (page 32)	1 recipe Mojito Glaze
2 Tbsp. finely chopped fresh mint leaves	Toppings: lime wedges, fresh mint sprigs

1. Prepare White Cake batter, stirring in 2 Tbsp. mint. Bake and cool as directed.

2. Pour about 2 Tbsp. Mojito Glaze over each cupcake. Top each with 1 lime wedge and 1 mint sprig.

mojito glaze

3 cups powdered sugar	1 tsp. lime zest
2 to 3 Tbsp. fresh lime juice	⅛ tsp. salt
1 to 2 Tbsp. rum	

1. Stir together all ingredients in a medium bowl until smooth. Add more lime juice or rum, if necessary, to make glaze pourable. Makes 1½ cups.

flip it!

St. Patty's Day

For a little luck o' the Irish, replace Mojito Glaze with Fresh Lime Frosting (page 106). Roll green fondant out to ⅛-inch thickness; cut out four-leaf clover shapes, and place on top of wet frosting. Roll edges of cupcakes in gold sparkling sugar, and top with a sprinkle of edible glitter.

Definitely for the adventurous, this spicy-sweet tidbit is a fiesta in your mouth. We combined Fresh Lime Frosting and dried mangos and added a smoldering kick from a little ground red pepper. Like a little more heat? Add extra pepper, but be careful—don't get burned.

flip it!
Day of the Dead

• This cupcake flip celebrates the traditional Mexican holiday that honors family and friends who have passed away. Omit the mango and red pepper. Tint the frosting dark green and red. Frost the cupcakes green, and pipe red designs on the edges using metal tip no. 3. Top each with a candy skull and candy flowers.

baker's secret

• Lime oil—an all-natural fruit flavor—is a remarkably intense essence cold pressed from the rind of fresh limes. We use Boyajian brand; if you want to sample these without purchasing a large bottle, a trio of 1-ounce bottles in lemon, lime, and orange flavors is available.

Mucho Gusto

makes 48 mini cupcakes

1	recipe White Cake (page 32)	Toppings: dried mango, ground
1	recipe Fresh Lime Frosting	red pepper

1. Prepare White Cake using 2 (24-cup) mini muffin pans lined with mini paper baking cups coated with cooking spray, filling each cup two-thirds full. Bake for 10 minutes or until a wooden pick inserted in center comes out clean; cool as directed.

2. Frost each cupcake with Fresh Lime Frosting. (See How-To, page 23.) Top each with 2 (¼–inch) strips dried mango, and sprinkle very lightly with red pepper.

fresh lime frosting

½	cup butter, softened	1	drop green liquid food coloring
¼	tsp. salt	1	tsp. lime zest,
1	tsp. lime oil		(optional)
¼	cup fresh lime juice (about	1	(16-oz.) package powdered
	1 lime)		sugar

1. Beat first 5 ingredients and, if desired, lime zest at medium speed with an electric mixer until creamy.

2. Gradually add powdered sugar, beating at low speed until blended. Beat at high speed 2 minutes or until creamy. Makes 3 cups.

One of the happiest events we celebrate is the arrival of a new baby. Whether boy or girl, it is always exciting. The newest craze is to reveal the sex of the baby by colored cake or filling hidden underneath a layer of white or chocolate frosting. When you take your first bite, the blue or pink announces the coming of a son or daughter. Sometimes we are the first to know. I love my job!

Oh Baby!

makes 24 cupcakes

1	recipe of your favorite cupcake flavor	Pink and blue food coloring gel
1	recipe Vanilla Frosting (page 33)	White sprinkles
		Toppings: candy baby shower decorations

1. Prepare cupcakes as directed.

2. Divide frosting into 2 bowls. Using food coloring gels, tint 1 bowl of frosting pale pink and 1 bowl of frosting pale blue, stirring until blended.

3. Frost 12 cupcakes pink and 12 cupcakes blue. (See How-To, page 23.) Roll edges of cupcakes in white sprinkles. Top with baby shower decorations. (We like onesies, baby faces, and baby booties.)

flip it!

Peek-a-Boo

• Here's how to hide the secret surprise of the baby's gender inside the Oh Baby! cakes. Fill cupcakes with pink- or blue-tinted Vanilla Frosting, so when they take a bite, everyone can celebrate the coming bundle of joy. Frost cupcakes smooth with white Vanilla Frosting. Insert metal tip no. 21 into a large decorating bag; fill bag with blue-tinted frosting. Pipe a blue border around cupcakes. Insert metal tip no. 3 into a large decorating bag; fill bag with pink-tinted frosting. Pipe pink question marks on top of cupcake, and sprinkle with edible glitter.

We just had to show our colors by using a vibrant wave of fresh fruit and the nickname for our beloved flag—Old Glory. We love the timeless lyrics George M. Cohan wrote so many years ago, "...the emblem of the land I love, the home of the free and the brave." Our heart beats true for this grand ol' cupcake.

Old Glory

makes 24 cupcakes

1	recipe Strawberry Cake (page 34)	1	pint fresh strawberries, sliced
3	cups Fresh Whipped Cream (page 63)	1	cup fresh blueberries

1. Prepare Strawberry Cake as directed.

2. Frost each cupcake with about 2 Tbsp. Fresh Whipped Cream. (See How-To, page 23.) Top each with 3 strawberry slices and 5 blueberries.

Right about the time spring is ending, we begin to count the days until the first crop of summer peaches arrive. We eat them, preserve them, and even store them to get us through until the next season. Dreamcakes' Peaches-and-Cream cupcake is a favorite every summer. Topped with a generous juicy peach slice, it is exceptional.

Peaches-and-Cream

makes 24 cupcakes

1	recipe White Cake (page 32)	1	cup Vanilla Frosting (page 33)
1	recipe Peach Frosting, divided		Fresh ripe peach slices

1. Prepare White Cake as directed.

2. Fill each cupcake using about 1½ cups Peach Frosting. (See How-To, page 21.)

3. Fold 1 cup Vanilla Frosting into remaining Peach Frosting, stirring gently until marbled.

4. Frost each cupcake with marbled frosting. (See How-To, page 23.) Top each with 1 peach slice just before serving.

peach frosting

2	large ripe peaches, peeled and chopped (about 1 cup)	5	cups powdered sugar
¾	cup butter, softened	⅛	tsp. salt

1. Process peaches in a blender or food processor until pureed. (Puree should measure about ½ cup.)

2. Beat butter and peach puree at medium speed with an electric mixer until creamy.

3. Gradually add powdered sugar and salt, beating at low speed until blended. Beat at high speed 2 minutes or until creamy. Makes 3 cups.

baker's secret

• Peach jam may be substituted for the filling, if desired. We prefer Stonewall Kitchen.

• Peach jam may be substituted for peach puree in the frosting when fresh peaches are unavailable.

Rumor has it that the Piña Colada was first introduced on August 16, in Puerto Rico. So it's only fitting that we pay tribute to the tasty blend as my daughter Katie's birthday is August 16. We're happy to celebrate any day with this luscious combination of pineapple and coconut. Katie also really loves the tiny umbrellas.

Piña Colada

makes 24 cupcakes

1	recipe Pineapple Cake	Toppings: yellow jumbo sprinkles,
1½	cups pineapple preserves	tiny drink umbrellas
1	recipe Coconut Cream Frosting	
	(page 38)	

1. Prepare Pineapple Cake as directed.

2. Fill each cupcake with pineapple preserves. (See How-To, page 21.)

3. Frost each cupcake with Coconut Cream Frosting. (See How-To, page 23.) Top each with yellow sprinkles and 1 drink umbrella.

pineapple cake

1	cup butter, softened	1	tsp. salt
2	cups sugar	1	cup frozen pineapple juice
4	large eggs		concentrate, thawed
3	cups all-purpose soft-wheat flour		Paper baking cups
2	tsp. baking powder		Vegetable cooking spray

1. Preheat oven to 350°.

2. Beat butter and sugar at medium speed with an electric mixer until creamy. Add eggs, 1 at a time, beating until blended after each addition.

3. Combine flour, baking powder, and salt; add to butter mixture alternately with pineapple juice, beginning and ending with flour mixture. Beat at low speed until blended after each addition.

flip it!

Pineapple-Orange

• Flip this drink-flavored favorite into a fresh Pineapple-Orange delight by filling each cupcake with orange marmalade. Frost each cupcake with Classic Orange Frosting (page 85) using metal tip no. 2D. Top each with orange sprinkles and a candy flower.

4. Place paper baking cups in 2 (12-cup) muffin pans, and coat with cooking spray; spoon batter into cups, filling two-thirds full.

5. Bake for 12 to 15 minutes or until a wooden pick inserted in center comes out clean. Cool in pans on wire racks 10 minutes; remove from pans to wire racks, and cool completely. Makes 24 cupcakes.

Tart and sweet, this lovely pink cupcake is fun to eat. We dust it with pink lemonade mix.

Pink Lemonade

makes 24 cupcakes

1   recipe Pink Lemonade Cake
1   recipe Pink Lemonade Frosting

Toppings: powdered pink lemonade mix, pink jumbo sprinkles, pink candies

1. Prepare Pink Lemonade Cake as directed.

2. Frost each cupcake with Pink Lemonade Frosting using metal tip no. 12. (See How-To, page 23.) Dust with pink lemonade mix, and top with pink sprinkles.

pink lemonade cake

1   cup butter, softened
1¾ cups sugar
¼   cup powdered pink lemonade mix
4   large eggs
3   cups all-purpose soft-wheat flour
2   tsp. baking powder
½   tsp. salt
¾   cup milk
Paper baking cups
Vegetable cooking spray

1. Preheat oven to 350°.

2. Beat butter, sugar, and lemonade mix at medium speed with an electric mixer until creamy. Add eggs, 1 at a time, beating until blended after each addition.

3. Combine flour, baking powder, and salt; add to butter mixture alternately with milk, beginning and ending with flour mixture. Beat at low speed until blended after each addition.

4. Place paper baking cups in 2 (12-cup) muffin pans, and coat with cooking spray; spoon batter into cups, filling two-thirds full.

5. Bake for 12 to 15 minutes or until a wooden pick inserted in center comes out clean. Cool in pans on wire racks 10 minutes; remove from pans to wire racks, and cool completely. Makes 24 cupcakes.

flip it!

Strawberry-Lemonade

• For a tasty twist, replace Pink Lemonade Frosting with a generous swirl of Strawberry Frosting, (page 42). Use metal tip no. 2D. Top each cupcake with yellow sprinkles and a candy lemon slice cut into 2 wedges.

baker's secret

• We pulse our lemonade mix in a blender or food processor about 10 times to make a fine powder.

pink lemonade frosting

¼   cup powdered pink lemonade mix

½   cup butter, softened

2   to 3 Tbsp. whipping cream

1   (16-oz.) package powdered sugar

1. Dissolve pink lemonade mix in 3 Tbsp. water. Beat butter, lemonade mixture, and whipping cream at medium speed with an electric mixer until creamy.

2. Gradually add powdered sugar, beating at low speed until blended. Beat at high speed 2 minutes or until creamy. Makes 3 cups.

You don't need a campfire to enjoy this cupcake. S'mores might just be the official dessert of summer, and you will definitely want some more once you've tasted these layers of graham crackers and marshmallows drenched in chocolate. Be sure to toast extra marshmallows because they seem to have a way of disappearing before making it to the cupcakes.

S'mores

makes 24 cupcakes

1   recipe Chocolate Cake (page 45)

1   recipe Vanilla Frosting (page 33)

24 jumbo-size marshmallows
Vegetable cooking spray

6   graham crackers, broken into large pieces

1   recipe Chocolate Ganache (page 39)

1. Prepare Chocolate Cake as directed.

2. Preheat broiler with oven rack 6 inches from heat.

3. Place marshmallows on an aluminum foil-lined baking sheet coated with cooking spray. Broil 3 to 4 minutes or until marshmallows are toasted to desired degree of doneness and color. Watch closely to avoid burning.

4. Fill each cupcake with Chocolate Ganache. (See How-To, page 21.)

5. Frost each cupcake with Vanilla Frosting. (See How-To, page 23.) Top each with graham cracker pieces, and drizzle with Chocolate Ganache. Place 1 toasted marshmallow on top of each cupcake.

Surf's up! Have fun in the sun with the sparkling sanding sugar and whimsical almond starfish that top our Sand Dollars. The color of waves and sand, these sunny cupcakes make your beach party another day in paradise.

Sand Dollars

makes 24 cupcakes

1 recipe Butter Cake (page 40)	Yellow and blue food coloring gel
1 recipe Wedding Cake Frosting (page 31)	White sanding sugar
	Pastel-colored Jordan Almonds

1. Prepare Butter Cake as directed.

2. Divide Wedding Cake Frosting into 2 bowls. Tint 1 bowl of frosting a pale yellow and 1 bowl of frosting a pale blue using food coloring gel. Frost 12 cupcakes yellow and 12 cupcakes blue. (See How-To, page 23.) Immediately sprinkle top of each cupcake with sanding sugar. Arrange 5 Jordan almonds into a starfish design on top of each cupcake.

baker's secret

• Once the frosting dries, sanding sugar won't adhere. Sprinkle the sugar immediately after frosting cupcakes.

flip it!
Christening Cakes

• For a beautiful cake to celebrate baptisms and christenings, omit Jordan Almonds and sparkling sugar. Tint Wedding Cake Frosting a pale green with liquid food coloring. Frost each cupcake smooth with frosting. Roll the edges of the cupcakes in white sprinkles. Pipe a cross on top using a small round piping tip and white Wedding Cake Frosting.

In the summer, I pick lavender blossoms and pin them to my apron to enjoy their fragrance as I work. Lavender lends a unique flavor and when combined with honey, it's sublime.

Sweet Lavender Cupcakes

makes 24 cupcakes

1   recipe Butter Cake (page 40)
1   recipe Wild Honey Frosting

Fresh lavender blossoms
1   recipe Lavender Brittle

1. Prepare Butter Cake as directed.

2. Frost each cupcake with Wild Honey Frosting using metal tip no. 12. (See How-To, page 23.) Top each with lavender blossoms and 1 piece Lavender Brittle.

wild honey frosting

½   cup butter, softened
8   oz. mascarpone cheese, softened
¼   cup wildflower honey

⅛   tsp. salt
1   (16-oz.) package powdered sugar

1. Beat first 4 ingredients at medium speed with a mixer until creamy.

2. Gradually add powdered sugar, beating at low speed until blended. Beat at high speed 2 minutes or until creamy. Makes 3 cups.

lavender brittle

Vegetable cooking spray
½   cup sugar

1   tsp. lavender

1. Line a baking sheet with heavy-duty foil; coat with cooking spray.

2. Combine sugar and ¼ cup water in a small saucepan. Cook over medium-high heat, stirring gently until sugar dissolves. Cook 4 minutes or until golden. (Do not stir.) Remove from heat; carefully stir in lavender. Rapidly spread mixture onto prepared baking sheet. Cool completely; break into pieces. Makes ½ cup.

flip it!

Bee Hive Cupcakes

• For a fun summertime flip, use metal tip no. 12 to pipe Wild Honey Frosting into a cone shape to mimic a bee hive. Replace lavender brittle with sugar honey bees and flowers.

baker's secret

• You can find the sugar honey bees and flowers for Bee Hive Cupcake at cakedeco.com.

A fat-free and satisfying cupcake, you ask? We have you covered. Fluffy Italian Meringue Frosting and light-as-a-cloud Angel Food Cake—so delicious you won't have any complaint, especially about your waistline.

White Cloud Cupcakes

makes 30 cupcakes

1   recipe Angel Food Cake
1   recipe Italian Meringue Frosting

Topping: fondant birds (optional)

1. Prepare Angel Food Cake as directed.

2. Split each cupcake in half; spoon bottom half of each with 2 Tbsp. Italian Meringue Frosting. Replace top half of each cupcake, and spoon an additional 2 Tbsp. frosting on top. Top with fondant birds, if desired.

angel food cake

1   cup all-purpose soft-wheat flour
½   cup powdered sugar
1   cup granulated sugar, divided
10 large egg whites
1   tsp. cream of tartar
½   tsp. salt

1   tsp. clear vanilla extract
2   tsp. fresh lemon juice
½   tsp. almond extract
    Paper baking cups
    Vegetable cooking spray

1. Preheat oven to 350°.

2. Combine flour and powdered sugar. Sift mixture into a medium bowl; repeat procedure. Whisk in ¼ cup granulated sugar; set aside.

3. Beat egg whites in a large bowl at high speed with an electric mixer until foamy. Add cream of tartar and salt, beating until soft peaks form. Gradually add remaining ¾ cup sugar, 2 Tbsp. at a time, beating until stiff peaks form and sugar dissolves. Add vanilla, lemon juice, and almond extract, beating until blended. Sprinkle flour mixture over egg white mixture, ¼ cup at a time, gently folding in after each addition.

4. Place 30 paper baking cups in 3 (12-cup) muffin pans, and coat with cooking spray; spoon batter into cups, filling two-thirds full.

5. Bake for 12 to 15 minutes or until a wooden pick inserted in center comes out clean. Cool in pans on wire racks 10 minutes; remove from pans to wire racks, and cool completely. Makes 30 cupcakes.

italian meringue frosting

3	large egg whites	¼	tsp. salt
½	tsp. cream of tartar	1	tsp. clear vanilla extract
¾	cup sugar	½	tsp. almond extract

1. Beat egg whites and cream of tartar in a large bowl at high speed with an electric mixer until soft peaks form.

2. Combine sugar, ¼ cup water, and salt in a small saucepan. Cook over medium heat, stirring frequently, until sugar dissolves; bring to a boil. Cook, without stirring, 2 minutes or until a candy thermometer registers 238° (soft ball stage). Pour hot syrup in a thin stream over egg whites, beating at high speed until stiff peaks form. Stir in vanilla and almond extracts. Makes 4 to 5 cups.

White Linen cupcakes are a light creation of Mascarpone Frosting and white chocolate curls over a tender cupcake. Serve it with an ice-cold glass of milk.

White Linen

makes 24 cupcakes

1	recipe Vanilla Bean Cake	White chocolate curls
1	recipe Mascarpone Frosting (page 145)	

1. Prepare Vanilla Bean Cake as directed.
2. Frost each cupcake with Mascarpone Frosting. (See How-To, page 23.) Top each generously with white chocolate curls.

vanilla bean cake

½	cup butter, softened	2	tsp. baking powder
1	cup shortening	½	tsp. salt
2	cups sugar	1	cup buttermilk
4	large eggs	1	to 2 Tbsp. vanilla bean paste
2¾	cups all-purpose soft-wheat flour		Paper baking cups
			Vegetable cooking spray

1. Preheat oven to 350°.
2. Beat butter and shortening at medium speed with an electric mixer until creamy. Gradually add sugar, beating well. Add eggs, 1 at a time, beating until blended after each addition.
3. Combine flour, baking powder, and salt; add to butter mixture alternately with buttermilk, beginning and ending with flour mixture. Beat at low speed until blended after each addition. Stir in vanilla bean paste.
4. Place paper baking cups in 2 (12-cup) muffin pans, and coat with cooking spray; spoon batter into cups, filling about two-thirds full.
5. Bake for 12 to 15 minutes or until a wooden pick inserted in center comes out clean. Cool in pans on wire racks 10 minutes; remove from pans to wire racks, and cool completely. Makes 24 cupcakes.

baker's secret

• Chocolate curls make quite an impressive topping. Use a good quality milk chocolate or white chocolate bar without nuts or fillings. Soften it very slightly in the microwave about 10 seconds on HIGH; microwave again an extra 5 seconds at a time, if needed. Pull a sharp vegetable peeler along narrow end of bar, letting curls fall onto a chilled sheet pan. The secret is having the chocolate at just the right temperature and using gentle pressure with the vegetable peeler.

This is a real dandy. It would be a great addition to your July 4th celebration spread. The amusing effect of the swirled frosting can be duplicated using any colors for any occasion. It makes a fun Christmas cupcake using red and green or a pretty spring cupcake using pink and green.

Red, White, and Blue

makes 24 cupcakes

1   recipe White Cake (page 32)
1½ cups strawberry or blueberry jam
1   recipe Vanilla Frosting (page 33)

Red and blue food coloring gel
Toppings: red jumbo sprinkles, edible glitter stars, red candies, star picks (optional)

1. Prepare White Cake as directed.

2. Fill each cupcake with strawberry or blueberry jam. (See How-To, page 21.)

3. Divide frosting into 3 bowls. Tint 1 bowl of frosting with desired amount of red food coloring and 1 bowl of frosting with desired amount of blue food coloring.

4. Insert metal tip no. 2D into a large decorating bag; spoon ¼ cup each of red, white, and blue frosting into bag. Pipe a generous peak of frosting onto each cupcake. Top each with sprinkles, glitter stars, 1 red candy, and, if desired, 1 star pick.

This is another of our staff's favorite cupcakes—a dense, buttery shortcake topped with Fresh Whipped Cream and berries. We use strawberries, but it's just as delicious with blueberries or peaches or both! Our favorite way to eat these little cakes is broken in a bowl with a splash of cream, a dollop of Fresh Whipped Cream, and a sprinkle of crunchy sugar to top it all off.

flip it!

Choco-Cherry Shortcakes

• An easy addition and a quick substitution create an entirely different shortcake taste. Prepare cupcakes as directed, adding 1 cup semisweet chocolate morsels to the batter. Use metal tip no. 2D to pipe Fresh Whipped Cream onto each cupcake. Substitute cherries for strawberries.

Strawberry Shortcakes

makes 24 cupcakes

2½ cups all-purpose baking mix	Whipping cream (optional)
⅔ cup granulated sugar	1 recipe Fresh Whipped Cream (page 63)
1 cup whipping cream	
6 Tbsp. butter, melted	2 cups sliced fresh strawberries
Paper baking cups	Coarse sparkling sugar
Vegetable cooking spray	

1. Preheat oven to 425°.

2. Combine baking mix and granulated sugar in a large bowl; add cream and butter, stirring until a soft dough forms.

3. Place paper baking cups in 2 (12-cup) muffin pans, and coat with cooking spray; spoon batter into cups, filling two-thirds full. Sprinkle tops of each with sparkling sugar before baking.

4. Bake for 12 minutes or until golden brown. Cool in pans on wire racks 10 minutes; remove from pans to wire racks, and cool completely.

5. To serve, place 1 cupcake in a small bowl and top with a splash of whipping cream, if desired. Top with 2 to 3 Tbsp. Fresh Whipped Cream, sliced strawberries, and a sprinkle of sparkling sugar.

Note: We tested with Bisquick Original Pancake and Baking Mix.

One of our very first cupcakes and still a bestseller, Tutti Frutti was intended to delight children with all the brightly colored fruit candy. To our surprise, adults were buying them more than children. When they realized the candy topping was a childhood favorite, they couldn't wait; they immediately began eating it standing in front of the bakery case. Make this one right away—your childhood is calling!

Tutti Frutti

makes 24 cupcakes

1 recipe Strawberry Cake (page 34)

2 recipes Strawberry Frosting (page 42)

Fruit-flavored candy bits

flip it!

Crazy for Candy

1. Prepare Strawberry Cake as directed.

2. Fill each cupcake with Strawberry Frosting. (See How-To, page 21.)

3. Frost each cupcake with Strawberry Frosting. (See How-To, page 23.) Roll top of each cupcake in candy bits, completely covering the top.

Note: We tested with Nerds for the fruit-flavored candy bits.

• For another childhood favorite-flavor treat, replace the fruit-flavored candy bits with mini candy-coated chocolate pieces.

Fall Follies

After our lingering deep South summer, we welcome nippy autumn breezes, warm scarves, and the swirl of vibrantly colored leaves to inspire our festival of flavors...apple, caramel, pumpkin, and pecan. Here is a harvest of fall cupcakes to start the season.

Apple and caramel are pretty simple ingredients, but when combined they are a delectable treat. Top off these cupcakes with toasted pecans to create a traditional fall favorite. We love to add the tiny crab apples as a garnish for extra-special occasions.

Caramel Apple Cupcakes

makes 24 cupcakes

1   recipe Fresh Apple Cake (page 142)

1   recipe Old-Fashioned Caramel Frosting (page 67)

Toppings: toasted pecans, fresh crab apples (optional)

1. Prepare Fresh Apple Cake as directed.

2. Frost each cupcake with Old-Fashioned Caramel Frosting. (See How-To, page 23.) Top each with toasted pecans and, if desired, 1 fresh crab apple.

baker's secret

• Most of the time we toast pecans and other nuts before using them because toasting really brings out the flavor. You can toast them in a skillet over medium-high heat, tossing them until you begin to detect their aroma, or bake them at 350° about 4 to 5 minutes or until toasted, stirring occasionally.

Our Cornmeal Cupcakes are wonderful served warm in a pool of lemon glaze. It has a light crunch of cornmeal in a tender, mildly sweet cake.

Cornmeal Cupcakes with Fresh Lemon Glaze

makes 24 cupcakes

1⅓ cups all-purpose soft-wheat flour	⅓ cup olive oil or canola oil
1⅓ cups sugar	2 large eggs
½ cup plain yellow cornmeal	1 tsp. vanilla extract
½ tsp. baking soda	Paper baking cups
¼ tsp. baking powder	Vegetable cooking spray
½ tsp. salt	Fresh Lemon Glaze
1 cup buttermilk	Lemon zest (optional)

1. Preheat oven to 350°.

2. Combine flour and next 5 ingredients in a large bowl; make a well in center of mixture.

3. Whisk together buttermilk, oil, eggs, and vanilla; add to flour mixture, stirring just until moistened.

4. Place paper baking cups in 2 (12-cup) muffin pans, and coat with cooking spray; spoon batter into cups, filling two-thirds full.

5. Bake for 12 minutes or until a wooden pick inserted in center comes out clean. Cool in pans on wire racks 10 minutes; remove from pans to wire racks, and cool completely.

6. Pour Fresh Lemon Glaze over each cupcake. Top with lemon zest, if desired.

fresh lemon glaze

1 cup powdered sugar	2 to 3 Tbsp. fresh lemon juice

1. Combine powdered sugar and lemon juice, whisking until smooth. Makes ½ cup.

Don Vito is inspired by our love of The Godfather. This is a cupcake you can't refuse. Our version of Italian Cream Cake uses toasted walnuts, but toasted pecans would be just as nice.

Don Vito

makes 24 cupcakes

1	recipe Butter Cake (page 40)	1	recipe Don Vito Frosting
1	cup sweetened flaked coconut		Toasted walnuts
1	tsp. coconut extract		

1. Prepare Butter Cake batter; stir in coconut and extract. Bake and cool as directed.

2. Frost each cupcake with Don Vito Frosting. (See How-To, page 23.) Top each cupcake with 1 toasted walnut.

don vito frosting

1	recipe Cream Cheese Frosting (page 35)	1	cup finely chopped toasted walnuts
1	cup sweetened flaked coconut	½	tsp. coconut extract

1. Prepare Cream Cheese Frosting as directed. Add coconut, walnuts, and extract, stirring until blended. Makes 3 cups.

Our Fresh Apple Cake is a perfect combination of apples and spice. It can be eaten as is, but we love it hot from the oven then topped with Cheddar cheese and toasted walnuts.

Fresh Apple 'n' Cheddar Cupcakes

makes 24 cupcakes

1   recipe Fresh Apple Cake

24   Vermont sharp Cheddar cheese slices

Toasted walnut pieces (optional)

1. Prepare Fresh Apple Cake as directed; do not cool.

2. Top each cupcake while still warm with 1 cheese slice; top with walnuts, if desired.

fresh apple cake

½   cup butter, melted

1   cup granulated sugar

1   cup firmly packed dark brown sugar

2   large eggs

1   tsp. vanilla extract

2   cups all-purpose soft-wheat flour

1   tsp. baking soda

1   tsp. salt

2   tsp. ground cinnamon

4   large Granny Smith apples, peeled and chopped

Paper baking cups

Vegetable cooking spray

1. Preheat oven to 350°.

2. Stir together first 5 ingredients in a large bowl until blended.

3. Combine flour and next 3 ingredients; add to butter mixture, stirring until blended. Stir in apple.

4. Place paper baking cups in 2 (12-cup) muffin pans, and coat with cooking spray; spoon batter into cups, filling two-thirds full.

5. Bake for 12 to 15 minutes or until a wooden pick inserted in center comes out clean. Cool in pans on wire racks 10 minutes; remove from pans to wire racks, and cool completely. Makes 24 cupcakes.

Fresh figs and wildflower honey are two of my favorite things. Paired with Mascarpone Frosting, they make this an extravagant pleasure to eat as well as a beautiful treat to share with friends.

Honey and Fig Cupcakes

makes 24 cupcakes

1   recipe Butter Cake (page 40)
Fig preserves
1   recipe Mascarpone Frosting

Toppings: Halved fresh figs, warm honey

1. Prepare Butter Cake as directed.

2. Fill each cupcake with fig preserves. (See How-To, page 21.)

3. Frost each cupcake with Mascarpone Frosting. (See How-To, page 23.) Top each with 1 fig half, and drizzle with warm honey.

mascarpone frosting

1   cup whipping cream
12   oz. mascarpone cheese, softened

1   cup powdered sugar
1   tsp. vanilla extract
⅛   tsp. salt

1. Beat cream at high speed with an electric mixer until stiff peaks form.

2. Beat mascarpone, powdered sugar, vanilla, and salt in a large bowl at medium speed with mixer until blended. Gently fold whipped cream into mascarpone mixture until blended. Makes 3 cups.

Irish Cream is one of our most "manly" cupcakes. It's our take on a classic drink using Guinness Stout, Bailey's, and Irish whiskey. It isn't for sissies, but it's certainly delicious. For a version with less alcohol, you can omit the whiskey and use a nonalcoholic Irish coffee creamer in equal amounts. Much of the alcohol from the Guinness cooks out during baking, leaving a rich stout flavor to the cake.

Irish Cream

makes 24 cupcakes

1 pint Irish stout beer (2 cups)	1 tsp. baking powder
1 cup Dutch process cocoa or other good-quality cocoa	½ tsp. salt
1 cup butter, softened	1 tsp. chocolate extract or vanilla extract
2 cups superfine sugar or castor sugar	Paper baking cups
4 large eggs	Vegetable cooking spray
2¾ cups all-purpose soft-wheat flour	Irish Cream Frosting
1 tsp. baking soda	Toppings: edible glitter stars, brown candies

1. Preheat oven to 350°.

2. Stir together beer and cocoa in a large heavy saucepan over medium heat, and cook, stirring constantly, about 3 minutes or until mixture is smooth. Cool.

3. Beat butter at medium speed with an electric mixer until creamy; gradually add sugar, beating well. Add eggs, 1 at a time, beating until blended after each addition.

4. Combine flour and next 3 ingredients; add to butter mixture alternately with cocoa mixture, beginning and ending with cocoa mixture. Beat at low speed until blended after each addition. Stir in chocolate extract.

5. Place paper baking cups in 2 (12-cup) muffin pans, and coat with cooking spray; spoon batter into cups, filling two-thirds full.

6. Bake for 12 to 15 minutes or until a wooden pick inserted in center comes out clean. Cool in pans on wire racks 10 minutes; remove from pans to wire racks, and cool completely.

7. Frost each cupcake with Irish Cream Frosting using metal tip no. 2D. (See How-To, page 23.) Top each with glitter stars and 1 chocolate candy.

Note: We tested with Guinness for the Irish stout beer.

irish cream frosting

½	cup butter, softened	1	Tbsp. Irish whiskey (optional)
¼	tsp. salt	4	cups powdered sugar
⅓	cup Irish cream liqueur		

1. Beat butter, salt, liqueur, and, if desired, whiskey at medium speed with an electric mixer until creamy.

2. Gradually add powdered sugar, beating at low speed until blended. Beat at high speed 2 minutes or until creamy. Makes 3 cups.

Note: We used Bailey's for the Irish cream liqueur.

The first time I tasted Monkey Bread I thought, "This might be the best thing I have ever eaten." It has become a treasured family tradition; we have it for every holiday. We can hardly wait for it to cool enough to eat that first piece. The gooey, buttery cinnamon biscuits with the slightly crunchy edges bring an "mmmmm" every time! We recommend eating this one while it's still warm!!

Monkey Bread Jumbo Cupcakes

makes 24 jumbo cupcakes

3	(10-oz.) cans refrigerated buttermilk biscuits	⅓	cup orange juice
½	cup butter	2	tsp. ground cinnamon
2	cups firmly packed brown sugar		Jumbo paper baking cups
			Vegetable cooking spray

1. Preheat oven to 350°.

2. Cut each biscuit into four pieces; shape into balls.

3. Combine butter and next 3 ingredients in a small saucepan over medium heat. Bring to a boil; cook 1 minute. Remove from heat; let cool 5 minutes.

4. Dip each dough ball into syrup mixture.

5. Place paper baking cups in 4 (6-cup) jumbo muffin pans, and coat with cooking spray. Arrange balls evenly in baking cups, filling half way. Drizzle any remaining syrup over top.

6. Bake for 20 minutes or until done.

This cupcake is the showcase for our Halloween thrills. For the parade of goblins, ghosts, and monsters looking for something sweet, we top it with anything we can find on the candy aisle. There's no trick to this treat—it's scrumptious any time of year.

Trick or Treat

makes 24 cupcakes

1 cup butter, softened	2 tsp. baking powder
2 cups sugar	1 tsp. salt
4 large eggs	1 tsp. orange flavoring
½ cup milk	Paper baking cups
Zest of 1 orange, finely grated	Vegetable cooking spray
½ cup fresh orange juice (about 1 orange)	2 recipes Halloween Orange Frosting
3 drops orange liquid food coloring	Toppings: assorted candy, sprinkles, candy sticks
3 cups all-purpose soft-wheat flour	

1. Preheat oven to 350°.

2. Beat butter and sugar at medium speed with an electric mixer until creamy. Add eggs, 1 at a time, beating until blended after each addition.

3. Combine milk and next 3 ingredients in a small bowl.

4. Combine flour, baking powder, and salt; add to butter mixture alternately with milk mixture, beginning and ending with flour mixture. Beat at low speed until blended after each addition. Stir in orange flavoring.

5. Place paper baking cups in 2 (12-cup) muffin pans, and coat with cooking spray; spoon batter into cups, filling two-thirds full.

6. Bake for 12 to 15 minutes or until a wooden pick inserted in center comes out clean. Cool in pans on wire racks 10 minutes; remove from pans to wire racks, and cool completely.

7. Fill each cupcake with Halloween Orange Frosting. (See How-To, page 21.)

flip it!

Autumn Leaves

• A quick switch of decorations flips our feature cupcake into a season-long treat. All you have to do is replace the assorted candy and sprinkles with a cluster of colorful fondant maple leaves.

8. Frost each cupcake with Halloween Orange Frosting using metal tip no. 12. (See How-To, page 23.) Top each with assorted candy, sprinkles, and 1 candy stick.

halloween orange frosting

| 1 | recipe Classic Orange Frosting (page 85) | 1 | to 2 drops orange liquid food coloring |
| 3 | Tbsp. fresh orange juice | | |

1. Prepare Classic Orange Frosting as directed.

2. Add juice and food coloring; beat at low speed with an electric mixer until blended. Beat at high speed 2 minutes or until creamy. Makes 3 cups.

Chocolate and peanut butter—the perfect pairing. The generous swirl of Peanut Butter Frosting and luscious filling of Chocolate Ganache make this an irresistible chocolate treat.

Peanut Butter Cup

makes 24 cupcakes

1   recipe Chocolate Cake (page 45)

1   recipe Chocolate Ganache (page 39)

1   recipe Peanut Butter Frosting (page 183)

Toppings: Chocolate Ganache; miniature peanut butter cup candies, cut in half

1. Prepare Chocolate Cake as directed.

2. Fill each cupcake with Chocolate Ganache. (See How-To, page 21.)

3. Frost each cupcake with Peanut Butter Frosting using metal tip no. 12. (See How-To, page 23.) Drizzle each with warm Chocolate Ganache, and top with half of a peanut butter cup.

flip it!

Oh Nuts!

• For a delightfully crunchy variation, omit the Chocolate Ganache drizzle, and replace the miniature peanut butter cup candies with chocolate-covered peanuts.

Pecan Pie is the quintessential dessert of fall. Crunchy toasted pecans and buttery Piecrust Leaves enhance the rich creamy frosting for a cupcake you'll make again and again.

Pecan Pie Cupcakes

makes 24 cupcakes

1	recipe Butter Cake (page 40)	Toppings:	1 cup chopped toasted pecans, Piecrust Leaves
1	recipe Pecan Pie Frosting		

1. Prepare Butter Cake as directed.

2. Frost each cupcake with Pecan Pie Frosting. (See How-To, page 23.) Top each with toasted pecans and 1 piecrust leaf.

pecan pie frosting

1	cup firmly packed dark brown sugar	1	cup whipping cream
1	cup dark corn syrup	¼	tsp. salt
½	cup cornstarch	4	Tbsp. butter
4	egg yolks	1	tsp. vanilla extract

1. Whisk together first 6 ingredients in a heavy saucepan. Bring to a boil over medium heat, whisking constantly. Boil, whisking constantly, 1 minute or until thickened.

2. Remove pan from heat; stir in butter and vanilla, whisking until butter melts. Place a sheet of plastic wrap directly on surface of mixture (to prevent a film from forming); chill about 3 hours or until thick. Makes 4 cups.

piecrust leaves

½ (14.1-oz.) package refrigerated piecrusts

1. Unroll piecrust on a flat surface. Using a ½-inch leaf cookie cutter, cut out leaves. Bake according to package directions. Makes about 48 leaves.

baker's secret

• Pecan Pie Frosting is best when made the night before.

When Pumpkin Patch Cupcakes are baking, the entire bakery fills with the fragrances of fall. This moist little cupcake is delicious and is the most beautiful golden pumpkin color.

Pumpkin Patch Cupcakes

makes 24 cupcakes

1   recipe Pumpkin Cake

2   recipes Cinnamon–Cream Cheese Frosting

Topping: multicolored sprinkles

Garnish: pumpkin picks

1. Prepare Pumpkin Cake as directed.

2. Fill each cupcake with Cinnamon–Cream Cheese Frosting. (See How-To, page 21.)

3. Frost each cupcake with Cinnamon–Cream Cheese Frosting. (See How-To, page 23.) Top each with sprinkles, and garnish with 1 pumpkin pick.

pumpkin cake

1½ cups butter, softened

2½ cups sugar

5   large eggs

1   cup canned pumpkin

1¾ cups all-purpose soft-wheat flour

1   tsp. baking powder

1   tsp. pumpkin pie spice

½   tsp. salt

⅔   cup buttermilk

1   tsp. vanilla extract

Paper baking cups

Vegetable cooking spray

1. Preheat oven to 350°.

2. Beat butter and sugar at medium speed with an electric mixer until creamy. Add eggs, 1 at a time, beating until blended after each addition. Add pumpkin, beating until blended.

3. Combine flour, baking powder, pumpkin pie spice, and salt; add to butter mixture alternately with buttermilk, beginning and ending with flour mixture. Beat at low speed until blended after each addition. Stir in vanilla.

4. Place paper baking cups in 2 (12-cup) muffin pans, and coat with cooking spray; spoon batter into cups, filling about two-thirds full.

baker's secret

• We top these little cakes off with paper pumpkins on a pick, but if you prefer an edible topping, look around the candy aisle for all sorts of pumpkin-shaped candies available in season.

5. Bake for 18 minutes or until a wooden pick inserted in center comes out clean. Cool in pans on wire racks 10 minutes; remove from pans to wire racks, and cool completely. Makes 24 cupcakes.

cinnamon–cream cheese frosting

1 recipe Cream Cheese Frosting (page 35) ½ tsp. ground cinnamon

1. Prepare Cream Cheese Frosting as directed. Add cinnamon, beating at low speed until blended. Beat at high speed 2 minutes or until creamy. Makes 3 cups.

This cupcake is inspired by a classic dessert from the '50s that was created at the famous Brennan's restaurant in New Orleans and is now served all over the South. It's a luscious combination of banana cake and creamy frosting with a drizzle of caramel. The only thing missing is the rum flambé!

Bananas Foster

makes 24 cupcakes

1   recipe Banana Cake (page 48)
1   recipe Vanilla Bean Frosting
     (page 37)
1   recipe Browned Butter Frosting
     (page 221)

Toppings: Caramel Drizzle (page 51), dried banana chips, turbinado sugar

1. Prepare Banana Cake as directed.

2. Fill each cupcake with Vanilla Bean Frosting. (See How-To, page 21.)

3. Frost each cupcake with Browned Butter Frosting. (See How-To, page 23.) Top each with Caramel Drizzle, 1 banana chip, and a sprinkle of turbinado sugar.

Popcorn balls bring back fun, fall memories. My mother's friend Beverly used to make them every Halloween. I watched with fascination as she poured the caramel over the freshly popped corn, formed the mixture into generous, apple-sized balls, and then carefully wrapped them in brightly colored Halloween bags for the trick-or-treaters who rang the doorbell. You can be sure I was one of the first, because I didn't want to miss out on that salty-sweet, crunchy, caramel goodness. At the bakery, we buy several kinds of caramel corn, and toss them together before topping our cupcakes. I like the different colors and textures you get by mixing several kinds.

Caramel Corn Crunch

makes 24 cupcakes

1	recipe Chocolate Cake (page 45)	3	cups caramel corn
1	recipe Old-Fashioned Caramel Frosting (page 67)		

1. Prepare Chocolate Cake as directed.

2. Frost each cupcake with Old-Fashioned Caramel Frosting. (See How-To, page 23.) Immediately cover each with caramel corn.

At Dreamcakes, we have a saying that anything tastes better with cream cheese. We go through several pounds of cream cheese each day. Our cheesecake cupcakes are simply amazing. They fly out of the bakery case whenever we make them. Chocolate and cream cheese—what could be better?

Chocolate Cheesecake

makes 24 cupcakes

1   recipe Chocolate Cake (page 45)
2   recipes Cream Cheese Frosting (page 35)

Chocolate curls (see Baker's Secret, page 126)

1. Prepare Chocolate Cake as directed.
2. Fill each cupcake with Cream Cheese Frosting. (See How-To, page 21.)
3. Frost each cupcake with Cream Cheese Frosting. (See How-To, page 23.) Top each with chocolate curls.

chocolate–cream cheese frosting

1   (8-oz.) package cream cheese, softened
½   cup butter, softened
1   tsp. vanilla extract
¼   tsp. salt

1   (16-oz.) package powdered sugar
⅓   cup unsweetened cocoa
¼   cup whipping cream

1. Beat first 4 ingredients at medium speed with an electric mixer until creamy.
2. Combine powdered sugar and cocoa; gradually add to cream cheese mixture alternately with cream, beginning and ending with powdered sugar mixture. Beat at low speed until blended after each addition. Beat at high speed 2 minutes or until creamy. Makes 3 cups.
Note: Use this frosting for our Chocolate–Chocolate Cheesecake version; see *flip it!* (at right).

flip it!

Chocolate–Chocolate Cheesecake

• Multiply the rich chocolate sensation times two by frosting the Chocolate Cheesecake cupcake with Chocolate–Cream Cheese Frosting (see recipe at left) in place of regular Cream Cheese Frosting.

These enchanting little cupcakes are the next best thing to a real box of truffles and much easier to make. The toppings you can use are endless; we don't have the space to name them all. Our favorites are toffee and cookie crumbs, but toasted pecans add such a wonderful crunch. So many toppings, so little time!

Chocolate Truffles

makes 48 mini cupcakes

1 recipe Chocolate Cake (page 45)

1½ cups Chocolate Ganache (page 39)

Toppings: cookie crumbs, cocoa powder, chocolate jimmies, chocolate mint crumbles

1. Prepare Chocolate Cake using 2 (24-cup) mini muffin pans lined with mini paper baking cups coated with cooking spray, filling each cup two-thirds full. Bake for 10 minutes or until a wooden pick inserted in center comes out clean; cool as directed.

2. Heat ganache until warm and melted. Dip tops of cupcakes in ganache, and immediately sprinkle with your choice of toppings to completely cover tops.

This remarkable cupcake was a suggestion from one of our patrons. It was the winning entry for a new cupcake flavor, the prize being a dozen of the winner's favorite cupcakes. We all win once you sink your teeth into this cinnamon and caramel creation.

Cinnamon Sugar Mama

makes 24 cupcakes

1   recipe Butter Cake (page 40)

2   recipes Cinnamon-Sugar Frosting

Toppings: Caramel Drizzle (page 51), caramel candies

1. Prepare Butter Cake as directed.

2. Fill each cupcake with Cinnamon-Sugar Frosting. (See How-To, page 21.)

3. Frost each cupcake with Cinnamon-Sugar Frosting. (See How-To, page 23.) Top each with Caramel Drizzle and 1 caramel candy.

cinnamon-sugar frosting

½   cup butter, softened

¼   cup whipping cream

2   tsp. ground cinnamon

⅛   tsp. salt

1   (16-oz.) package powdered sugar

1. Beat first 4 ingredients at medium speed with an electric mixer until creamy.

2. Gradually add powdered sugar, beating at low speed until blended. Beat at high speed 2 minutes or until creamy. Makes 3 cups.

flip it!

King Cake

• For festive cupcakes worthy of a Mardi Gras celebration, replace the Caramel Drizzle with a sprinkling of purple, green, and gold sparkling sugar. Place a King Cake traditional tiny plastic baby on top. (Be sure to remove the plastic baby before eating the cupcake.) *Laissez les bons temps rouler!*

This cupcake is a combination of all the best ingredients. I could eat the Coconut-Pecan Topping with a spoon. The caramel center and buttery frosting along with the tender chocolate cake is dangerously good and impossible to resist. It makes a really impressive presentation whether they are large or mini cupcakes, especially if you use the large chunky shards of coconut.

Completely Nuts

makes 48 mini cupcakes

1   recipe Chocolate Cake (page 45)

1   recipe Caramel Drizzle (page 51)

1   recipe Old-Fashioned Caramel Frosting (page 67)

1   recipe Coconut-Pecan Topping

1. Prepare Chocolate Cake using 2 (24-cup) mini muffin pans lined with mini paper baking cups coated with cooking spray, filling each cup two-thirds full. Bake for 10 minutes or until a wooden pick inserted in center comes out clean; cool as directed.

2. Fill each cupcake with Caramel Drizzle. (See How-To, page 21.)

3. Frost each cupcake with Old-Fashioned Caramel Frosting. (See How-To, page 23.) Top each with Coconut-Pecan Topping.

coconut-pecan topping

1   cup chopped toasted pecans

2   cups sweetened shredded coconut, toasted

1. Stir together pecans and coconut in a large bowl. Store any remaining topping in an airtight container for up to 2 weeks. Makes 3 cups.

flip it!

English Toffee

• Add a flavorful hint reminiscent of merry old England by replacing Coconut-Pecan Topping with a mix of toffee bits and chocolate mini-morsels.

The beginning of football season is so exciting, and showing your school spirit by decorating cupcakes in your team's colors is always fun. Depending on your favorite cupcake flavor, fill them with chocolate, caramel, or frosting. I'm a huge Brett Favre fan, so my Favre Fever cupcakes are green and gold and purple and gold. Go Team!

Football Fever

makes 24 cupcakes

1	recipe of your favorite cupcake flavor	Liquid food coloring (in your team's colors)
2	recipes Vanilla Frosting (page 33)	Toppings: assorted colored sprinkles, sugar footballs

1. Prepare cupcakes as directed.

2. Tint Vanilla Frosting using liquid food coloring.

3. Fill each cupcake with tinted frosting. (See How-To, page 21.)

4. Frost each cupcake with tinted frosting. (See How-To, page 23.) Top each with coordinating colored sprinkles and 1 sugar football.

baker's secret

• You can find the sugar footballs for Football Fever at cakedeco.com.

This cupcake is without a doubt most men's favorite. You can see the smile as soon as they spot that crisp bacon strip resting on top of the golden maple frosting. Once again, it's the wonderful combination of salty and sweet together. We describe it as the flavor you get when bacon mingles with syrup while eating pancakes. We suggest about half a slice on each cupcake, but feel free to add as much as you want.

Maple Bacon

makes 24 cupcakes

1   recipe Butter Cake (page 40)
1   recipe Maple Frosting

12   cooked bacon slices, broken
       to pieces

1. Prepare Butter Cake as directed.

2. Frost each cupcake with Maple Frosting using metal tip no. 2D. (See How-To, page 23.) Top each with bacon.

maple frosting

1   cup butter
1   (16-oz.) package dark brown
     sugar
½   cup evaporated milk
¼   tsp. baking soda

1   Tbsp. light corn syrup
4   cups powdered sugar
2   tsp. maple flavoring

1. Melt butter in a heavy saucepan over medium heat. Add brown sugar; bring to a boil, stirring constantly. Stir in evaporated milk, baking soda, and corn syrup; bring to a boil, stirring occasionally. Remove from heat, and let cool. Transfer caramel mixture to a large bowl.

2. Gradually add powdered sugar to caramel mixture; beat at medium speed with an electric mixer until creamy. Stir in maple flavoring. Beat at high speed 2 minutes or until creamy. Icing firms up quickly, so use immediately. Makes 3 cups.

flip it!

Maple Nut

• Flip this recipe to a nutty version by replacing the bacon with toasted or candied walnuts or pecans.

baker's secret

• The baking soda in the frosting helps prevent the caramel from becoming grainy.

Some days there is nothing more satisfying than a good old peanut butter and jelly sandwich. Thinking about it with really tart strawberry preserves makes my mouth water. Lunch Lady is just that, but in cupcake form. It is filled and drizzled with a sticky strawberry jam, and the Peanut Butter Frosting is melt-in-your-mouth good. Oh my, that burst of flavors just can't be beat.

Lunch Lady

makes 24 cupcakes

1   recipe Butter Cake (page 40)
2   cups strawberry jam or
    preserves, divided
1   recipe Peanut Butter Frosting
    (page 183)

Toppings: white sprinkles, red
    candies

1. Prepare Butter Cake as directed.

2. Fill each cupcakes using 1½ cups strawberry jam or preserves. (See How-To, page 21.)

3. Frost each cupcake with Peanut Butter Frosting using metal tip no. 12. (See How-To, page 23.)

4. Melt remaining ½ cup strawberry jam, and drizzle over each cupcake. Top with white sprinkles and 1 red candy.

If you are born in Alabama, one of the first things you proclaim as soon as you can talk is either "Roll Tide" or "War Eagle." Dream-cakes doesn't take sides; we think they are both champions—just like these winning cupcakes.

Roll Tide Red Velvet vs. Aubie Orange

Roll Tide Red Velvet

½	cup butter, softened	1	cup buttermilk
½	cup shortening	1	Tbsp. white vinegar
2	cups sugar	1	tsp. vanilla extract
3	large eggs		Paper baking cups
3	Tbsp. unsweetened cocoa		Vegetable cooking spray
2	oz. red liquid food coloring	1	recipe Cream Cheese
2	cups all-purpose soft-wheat flour		Frosting (page 35)
1	tsp. baking soda		Toppings: red sprinkles, sugar footballs, fondant elephants
½	tsp. salt		

1. Preheat oven to 350°.

2. Beat butter, shortening, and sugar at medium speed with an electric mixer until creamy. Add eggs, 1 at a time, beating until blended after each addition.

3. Stir together cocoa and food coloring, making a paste; add paste to butter mixture, beating until well blended.

4. Combine flour, baking soda, and salt in a small bowl. Whisk together buttermilk and vinegar in a separate bowl. Add flour mixture to butter mixture alternately with buttermilk mixture, beginning and ending with flour mixture. Beat at low speed until blended after each addition. Stir in vanilla.

5. Place paper baking cups in 2 (24-cup) mini muffin pans, and coat with cooking spray; spoon batter into cups, filling two-thirds full.

6. Bake for 10 minutes or until a wooden pick inserted in center comes out clean. Cool in pans on wire racks 10 minutes; remove from pans to wire racks, and cool completely.

7. Frost each cupcake with Cream Cheese Frosting using metal tip no. 2D. (See How-To, page 23.) Top each with red sprinkles and either 1 sugar football or 1 fondant elephant. Makes 48 mini cupcakes.

Aubie Orange

1 recipe White Cake (page 32)
2 recipes Halloween Orange
   Frosting (page 151)

Toppings: blue sprinkles, sugar
   footballs, fondant tigers

1. Prepare White Cake using 2 (24-cup) mini muffin pans lined with mini paper baking cups coated with cooking spray, filling each cup two-thirds full. Bake for 10 minutes or until a wooden pick inserted in center comes out clean; cool as directed.

2. Fill each cupcake with Halloween Orange Frosting. (See How-To, page 21.)

3. Frost each cupcake with Halloween Orange Frosting using metal tip no. 2D. (See How-To, page 23.) Top each with blue sprinkles and either 1 sugar football or 1 fondant tiger. Makes 48 mini cupcakes.

baker's secret

• We use circus-themed cookie cutters to cut out the fondant elephants and tigers for these cupcakes. Check the cake decorating aisle at your local crafts or hobby store for a variety of cookie cutter options for your team's mascot.

flip it!
Halloween Cupcakes

• If your thoughts of autumn are more about Halloween than football, flip this cupcake in that direction by replacing the footballs, tigers, and sprinkles with candy corn and decorative Halloween picks.

Nothing can top our Wizard's Hat cupcakes. They're a "sorting cap" for cupcake lovers—the inner flavor is revealed in the first magical bite.

Wizard's Hat

makes 24 cupcakes

1	recipe Chocolate Cake (page 45)	2	cups Mint Frosting (page 46)
2	cups Strawberry Frosting (page 42)	2	cups Vanilla Bean Frosting (page 37), tinted blue
2	cups Peanut Butter Frosting (page 183)	3	cups Chocolate Ganache, melted (page 39)
			Edible glitter stars

1. Prepare Chocolate Cake as directed.

2. Insert a metal tip no. 12 into each of 4 large decorating bags; fill each with a different flavor frosting. Pipe 1 flavor of frosting into a cone shape on top of 6 cupcakes. Repeat with remaining frostings and cupcakes. Place cupcakes in freezer for 10 to 15 minutes to harden frosting. Remove from freezer, and immediately dip tops into melted Chocolate Ganache, completely covering frosting. Sprinkle with glitter stars. Let stand until chocolate is set.

baker's secret

• If you don't have 4 no. 12 piping tips, assemble the decorating bags using decorating couplers to allow you to easily use the same tip on subsequent bags. You can also fill and pipe the 4 bags, one at a time.

• You'll need to make 1½ recipes of the Chocolate Ganache to have enough for dipping the Wizard's Hats. The 4 recipes for different frostings each yield 3 cups, so you'll have about a cup left over from each recipe. Bake a batch of cupcakes with the Butter Cake recipe (page 40) to use up the extra frosting, and set out a rainbow of cupcakes another day.

Another cupcake inspired by a much-loved dessert is our Tiramisu. If you can't have the actual tiramisu dessert, this is the next best thing. A rich, creamy coffee filling with a dusting of cocoa on top is the perfect afternoon pick-me-up, and it's not too sweet. This recipe is highly requested for weddings and parties.

Tiramisu

makes 24 cupcakes

1	recipe Butter Cake (page 40)		Unsweetened cocoa
1	recipe Tiramisu Filling		
1	recipe Cream Cheese Frosting (page 35)		

1. Prepare Butter Cake as directed.

2. Cut tops off cupcakes using a serrated knife. Spread about 1 Tbsp. Tiramisu Filling on bottom part of each cupcake; replace tops.

3. Frost each cupcake with Cream Cheese Frosting. (See How-To, page 23.) Dust each with cocoa.

tiramisu filling

1	(8-oz.) package cream cheese, softened	2	to 3 Tbsp. coffee liqueur or 1 Tbsp. coffee extract
⅓	cup powdered sugar	⅛	tsp. salt

1. Combine all ingredients in a medium bowl, stirring until well blended. Store any remaining filling in an airtight container in refrigerator for up to 1 week. Makes 2 cups.

Note: We tested with Kahlúa for the coffee liqueur.

Peanut Butter and Banana is a classic combo enjoyed by young and old alike. Moist banana cake and creamy Peanut Butter Frosting make it a customer and staff favorite, and we top it off with a banana-shaped candy for fun. We think Elvis would approve of this one.

Peanut Butter and Banana

makes 24 cupcakes

1   recipe Banana Cake (page 48)   Banana-shaped candies (optional)
1   recipe Peanut Butter Frosting

1. Prepare Banana Cake as directed.

2. Frost each cupcake with Peanut Butter Frosting using metal tip no. 12. (See How-To, page 23.) Top each with banana candies, if desired.

Note: We tested with Runts for the banana-shaped candies.

peanut butter frosting

½   cup butter, softened   4   cups powdered sugar
1   cup creamy peanut butter   ¼   to ½ cup whipping cream

1. Beat butter and peanut butter at medium speed with an electric mixer until creamy. Gradually add half of powdered sugar, beating at low speed until blended. Add ¼ cup cream, beating until creamy. Add remaining powdered sugar, beating until blended. If necessary, add more cream, beating at high speed 2 minutes or until creamy. Makes 3 cups.

flip it!

Chocolate Banana

• To create another classic flavor combination, replace the Peanut Butter Frosting with our Chocolate Frosting (page 41). Top cupcakes with dried banana chips and jumbo yellow sprinkles.

Chocolate High is all about chocolate. We tried to get as much of it as possible into one cupcake. This creation has turned out to be our staff chocoholic's favorite. With nothing but chocolate through and through, it's so beautiful piled high with Chocolate Frosting and Chocolate Ganache.

Chocolate High

makes 24 cupcakes

1	recipe Chocolate Cake (page 45)	1	recipe Chocolate Frosting (page 41)
1	recipe Chocolate Ganache (page 39)		Toppings: Chocolate Ganache, malted milk balls

1. Prepare Chocolate Cake as directed.

2. Fill each cupcake with Chocolate Ganache. (See How-To, page 21.)

3. Frost each cupcake with Chocolate Frosting using metal tip no. 2D. (See How-To, page 23.) Drizzle each with warm Chocolate Ganache, and top with 1 malted milk ball.

flip it!

Turtle Cupcakes

• Who doesn't love chocolate turtle candies?! Try this flip for a chocolatey version of that favorite candy. Prepare Chocolate High as directed, drizzling with both Chocolate Ganache and Caramel Drizzle (page 51). Omit the malted milk balls and sprinkle each cupcake with chopped toasted pecans.

Winter Wonders

Tastes and traditions of the season fill our bakery cases; it's a beautiful sight to see. The wonderland of Christmas flavors such as peppermint, gingerbread, eggnog, and coconut are featured in our delightful treats all Winter long.

Merry Christmas

Any excuse to buy Medjool dates will do, and this recipe is a superb reason to buy extra. These plump, gooey dates make this cupcake spectacular inside and out.

Blind Date

makes 24 cupcakes

1   recipe Date Cake
1   recipe Orange–Cream Cheese Frosting

Sugared Dates

1. Prepare Date Cake as directed.

2. Frost each cupcake with Orange–Cream Cheese Frosting using metal tip no. 12. (See How-To, page 23.) Top each with Sugared Dates.

date cake

2   cups chopped dates
¼   cup orange juice
½   cup butter, softened
¾   cup firmly packed dark brown sugar
2   large eggs
1   tsp. vanilla extract
1   Tbsp. orange zest (about 2 oranges)
2   cups all-purpose soft-wheat flour

2   tsp. baking powder
½   tsp. baking soda
½   tsp. ground cinnamon
½   tsp. salt
¼   tsp. cardamom (optional)
¾   cup fresh orange juice (1 to 2 oranges)

Paper baking cups
Vegetable cooking spray

1. Preheat oven to 350°.

2. Combine dates and ¼ cup orange juice in a small bowl; set aside.

3. Beat butter and brown sugar at medium speed with an electric mixer until creamy. Add eggs, 1 at a time, beating until blended after each addition. Stir in vanilla and orange zest.

4. Combine flour, baking powder, baking soda, cinnamon, salt, and, if desired, cardamom; add to butter mixture alternately with orange juice, beginning and ending with flour mixture. Beat at low speed until blended after each addition. Add date and orange juice mixture, stirring just until combined.

5. Place paper baking cups in 2 (12-cup) muffin pans, and coat with cooking spray; spoon batter into cups, filling two-thirds full.

6. Bake for 12 to 15 minutes or until a wooden pick inserted in center comes out clean. Cool in pans on wire racks 10 minutes; remove from pans to wire racks, and cool completely. Makes 24 cupcakes.

orange–cream cheese frosting

1	recipe Cream Cheese Frosting (page 35)	1	tsp. orange flavoring
		1	tsp. orange zest

1. Prepare Cream Cheese Frosting as directed. Add flavoring and zest, stirring until well blended. Beat at high speed 2 minutes or until creamy. Makes 3 cups.

sugared dates

1 cup chopped dates   3 Tbsp. sugar

1. Toss together chopped dates and sugar until dates are well coated. Makes 1 cup.

Note: We tested with Medjool dates, but any high-quality date will work.

To add a little kick to the chocolate cake recipe, substitute ¼ cup of your favorite bourbon for part of the water. Topping the cupcake with Bourbon Whipped Cream makes it a little more sophisticated and less sweet. And as for our favorite bourbon, we have an ongoing argument over Woodford Reserve and Maker's Mark; we'll let you decide.

Bourbon Sweet Cream Cupcakes

makes 48 mini cupcakes

1	recipe Chocolate Cake (page 45)	1	recipe Bourbon Whipped Cream
1	recipe Chocolate Ganache (page 39)		Toppings: red and white sprinkles

1. Prepare Chocolate Cake using 2 (24-cup) mini muffin pans lined with mini paper baking cups coated with cooking spray, filling each cup two-thirds full. Bake for 10 minutes or until a wooden pick inserted in center comes out clean; cool as directed.

2. Fill each cupcake with Chocolate Ganache. (See How-To, page 21.)

3. Frost each cupcake with Bourbon Whipped Cream. (See How-To, page 23.) Top each with red and white sprinkles.

bourbon whipped cream

1	pt. whipping cream, chilled	½	cup powdered sugar
¼	cup bourbon		

1. Beat cream in a medium-size chilled bowl at high speed with an electric mixer until soft peaks form. Gradually add bourbon and powdered sugar, beating at high speed until stiff peaks form. Makes 3 cups.

flip it!
Peppermint Cream

• For a sweeter treat, substitute peppermint syrup for bourbon in the whipped cream recipe, and finish with a scattering of red and white sprinkles.

Christmas Carol is one cupcake that we look forward to every year. To save time, you can make the Candied Orange Peel in larger batches. The peel will keep in an airtight container about 3 weeks (if you manage to have it that long!); we're inclined to snack on it, so we're usually remaking it a couple of times a week.

Christmas Carol Cupcakes

makes 24 cupcakes

1   recipe Cranberry-Orange Cake
1   recipe Classic Orange
    Frosting (page 85)

Candied Orange Peel

1. Prepare Cranberry-Orange Cake as directed.
2. Frost each cupcake with Orange Frosting. (See How-To, page 23.) Top each with Candied Orange Peel.

cranberry-orange cake

1	cup dried cranberries	½	tsp. salt
¼	cup orange juice	½	cup fresh orange juice (about 1 orange)
½	cup butter, softened	1	tsp. vanilla extract
¾	cup sugar	1	Tbsp. orange zest
2	large eggs		Paper baking cups
1½	cups all-purpose soft-wheat flour		Vegetable cooking spray
1½	tsp. baking powder		

1. Preheat oven to 350°.
2. Combine cranberries and ¼ cup orange juice; soak 30 minutes. Drain and set aside.
3. Beat butter and sugar at medium speed with an electric mixer until creamy. Add eggs, 1 at a time, beating until blended after each addition.

4. Combine flour, baking powder, and salt; add to butter mixture alternately with ½ cup orange juice, beginning and ending with flour mixture. Beat at low speed until blended after each addition. Stir in vanilla, orange zest, and reserved cranberries.

5. Place paper baking cups in 2 (12-cup) muffin pans, and coat with cooking spray; spoon batter into cups, filling two-thirds full.

6. Bake 12 to 15 minutes or until a wooden pick inserted in center comes out clean. Cool in pans on wire racks 10 minutes; remove from pans to wire racks, and cool completely. Makes 24 regular cupackes.

candied orange peel

3 large navel oranges	1½ cups sugar, divided
½ tsp. salt	¼ cup light corn syrup

1. Slice off ends of oranges. Using a vegetable peeler, cut the orange part of the peel from stem end of orange down to navel end, forming long ¾- to 1-inch-wide strips. Slice peel lengthwise into julienne strips.

2. Cook peel in a medium pot of boiling water 10 minutes or until tender. Remove peel with a slotted spoon; place on paper towels in a single layer to dry for about 10 minutes.

3. Bring salt, 1 cup sugar, corn syrup, and 1 cup water to a boil in a medium saucepan over high heat, stirring to dissolve sugar. Add peel, and boil 8 to 10 minutes or until it turns translucent and syrup thickens. Remove from heat. Transfer peel to a wire rack using a slotted spoon, separating pieces as needed. Let peel dry 1 hour. Toss with remaining ½ cup sugar to coat. Makes about ½ cup.

Note: Store in an airtight container at room temperature up to 3 weeks.

I love this fun version of cupcakes. These make great gifts or treats for children's parties. You can make them large or small, depending on your cookie cutter. The white chocolate added to the cereal mixture makes them sturdy and tastes great! We have so much fun decorating these that we fight over who gets to make them.

Crispy Marshmallow Cupcakes

makes 12 cupcakes

4	Tbsp. butter
4	(1-oz.) vanilla almond bark candy coating squares
4	cups miniature strawberry marshmallows
6	cups crisp rice cereal
	Vegetable cooking spray

2   (1-oz.) vanilla or chocolate almond bark candy coating squares, melted

Toppings: assorted sprinkles, chocolate candies, melted chocolate candy coating (optional)

1. Melt butter and vanilla candy coating in a large saucepan over low heat. Add marshmallows, and stir until completely melted. Remove from heat.

2. Add cereal to marshmallow mixture, stirring until well coated.

3. Line a 13- x 9-inch pan with wax paper, and coat with cooking spray. Using a buttered spatula or wax paper, press cereal mixture into prepared pan. Cool mixture completely. Remove from pan.

4. Cut out crispy cupcakes using a 3-inch cupcake-shaped cookie cutter. Dip tops of each cupcake in melted vanilla or chocolate candy coating. Top each immediately with sprinkles, 1 chocolate candy, and, if desired, drizzles of melted chocolate candy coating. Let coating set.

Note: Regular marshmallows may be used, if desired.

flip it!

Marshmallow Pops

• Ok, so technically it's not a cupcake, but it's too fun not to try. Insert a lollipop stick in the bottom of a large marshmallow. Dip the marshmallow in melted chocolate candy coating; let it set. Dip the top of the marshmallow in melted vanilla candy coating. Top immediately with colored sprinkles and a candy berry.

Serving eggnog can be tricky. Do you add the brandy or not? We think, "Yes, definitely!" Freshly grated nutmeg makes this cupcake exceptional.

Eggnog Cupcakes

makes 24 cupcakes

1 recipe Eggnog Cake	Toppings: freshly grated nutmeg,
2 recipes Eggnog Frosting	chocolate candies

1. Prepare Eggnog Cake as directed.
2. Fill each cupcake with Eggnog Frosting. (See How-To, page 21.)
3. Frost each cupcake with Eggnog Frosting using metal tip no. 12. (See How-To, page 23.) Top each with freshly grated nutmeg and 1 chocolate candy.

eggnog cake

½	cup butter, softened	½	tsp. freshly grated nutmeg
1½	cups sugar	¼	tsp. salt
3	large eggs	¾	cup refrigerated eggnog
1½	cups all-purpose soft-wheat flour	1	tsp. vanilla extract
			Paper baking cups
1	tsp. baking powder		Vegetable cooking spray

1. Preheat oven to 350°.
2. Beat butter at medium speed with an electric mixer until creamy; gradually add sugar, beating well. Add eggs, 1 at a time, beating until blended after each addition.
3. Combine flour, baking powder, nutmeg, and salt; add to butter mixture alternately with eggnog, beginning and ending with flour mixture. Beat at low speed until blended after each addition. Stir in vanilla.
4. Place paper baking cups in 2 (12-cup) muffin pans, and coat with cooking spray; spoon batter into cups, filling two-thirds full.
5. Bake for 12 to 15 minutes or until a wooden pick inserted in center comes out clean. Cool in pans on wire racks 10 minutes; remove from pans to wire racks, and cool completely. Makes 24 cupcakes.

eggnog frosting

½ cup butter, softened
⅓ cup refrigerated eggnog
2 Tbsp. brandy or 1 tsp. vanilla
   extract

⅛ tsp. salt
1 (16-oz.) package powdered
   sugar

1. Beat first 4 ingredients at medium speed with an electric mixer until creamy.

2. Gradually add powdered sugar, beating at low speed until blended. Beat at high speed 2 minutes or until creamy. Makes 3 cups.

As sweet as love's first kiss, our chocolate and cherry cupcake is special. One bite and you'll fall in love, all with a cherry on top!

First Kiss

makes 24 cupcakes

1	recipe Chocolate Cake (page 45)	24	red maraschino cherries (with stems)
24	milk chocolate kisses		Chocolate Ganache (page 39)
1	recipe Cherry Frosting		

1. Prepare Chocolate Cake as directed; do not cool.

2. While cupcakes are still warm, press 1 chocolate kiss into the center of each. Let cool completely.

3. Frost each cupcake with Cherry Frosting using metal tip no. 2D. (See How-To, page 23.)

4. Dip cherries in Chocolate Ganache, and place 1 on top of each cupcake.

cherry frosting

½	cup butter, softened	½	tsp. almond extract
3	Tbsp. cherry jam or maraschino cherry juice	⅛	tsp. salt
¼	cup whipping cream	1	(16-oz.) package powdered sugar

1. Beat first 5 ingredients at medium speed with an electric mixer until creamy.

2. Gradually add powdered sugar, beating at low speed until blended. Beat at high speed 2 minutes or until creamy. Makes 3 cups.

Our Gingerbread Cupcakes are a deliciously festive dessert. The classic blend of molasses and spices makes this moist cupcake a Christmas tradition at Dreamcakes. The melted frosting poured over the top is a perfect canvas for your favorite Christmas sprinkles.

Gingerbread Cupcakes

makes 36 cupcakes

1	cup water	1	Tbsp. baking powder
1	cup dark molasses	2	tsp. ground cinnamon
1	tsp. baking soda	2	tsp. dried ground ginger
½	cup cold water	½	tsp. salt
½	cup butter, softened	¼	tsp. ground cloves
1	cup firmly packed dark brown sugar		Paper baking cups
2	large eggs		Vegetable cooking spray
2½	cups all-purpose soft-wheat flour	1	recipe Cream Cheese Frosting (page 35)
			Red sprinkles (optional)

1. Preheat oven to 350°.

2. Bring 1 cup water to a boil in a 2-qt. saucepan over high heat. Remove from heat, and stir in molasses and baking soda. When mixture stops foaming, stir in ½ cup cold water. Cool.

3. Beat butter and brown sugar at medium speed with a mixer until creamy. Add eggs, 1 at a time, beating until blended after each addition.

4. Combine flour and next 5 ingredients; add to butter mixture alternately with molasses mixture, beginning and ending with flour mixture. Beat at low speed until blended after each addition.

5. Place paper baking cups in 3 (12-cup) muffin pans, and coat with cooking spray; spoon batter into cups, filling two-thirds full.

6. Bake for 12 to 15 minutes or until a wooden pick inserted in center comes out clean. Cool in pans on wire racks 10 minutes; remove from pans to wire racks, and cool completely.

7. Microwave Cream Cheese Frosting in a microwave-safe bowl at HIGH 1 minute or until melted. Stir with a whisk, and pour frosting over top of each cupcake. Top each with red sprinkles, if desired.

If you can't find gluten-free all-purpose flour, a good substitution is rice flour, soy flour, and tapioca flour in equal parts. Bob's Red Mill makes a wonderful gluten-free flour that can be found in most grocery stores and can also be ordered online.

Gluten-Free Cupcakes

makes 24 cupcakes

½	cup unsweetened cocoa	½	cup buttermilk
1	cup boiling water	2	tsp. chocolate extract or vanilla extract
1	cup butter, softened		Paper baking cups
2	cups sugar		Vegetable cooking spray
2	large eggs	1	recipe Vanilla Frosting (page 33)
2	cups gluten-free all-purpose flour		Food coloring gel in your favorite colors
1	tsp. baking soda		
½	tsp. salt		

1. Preheat oven to 350°.

2. Combine cocoa and 1 cup boiling water, stirring until blended and smooth; let cool.

3. Beat butter at medium speed with an electric mixer until creamy; gradually add sugar, beating well. Add eggs, 1 at a time, beating until blended after each addition. Add cocoa mixture, beating until blended.

4. Combine flour, baking soda, and salt; add to butter mixture alternately with buttermilk, beginning and ending with flour mixture. Beat at low speed until blended after each addition. Stir in chocolate extract.

5. Place paper baking cups in 2 (12-cup) muffin pans, and coat with cooking spray; spoon batter into cups, filling two-thirds full.

6. Bake for 12 to 15 minutes or until a wooden pick inserted in center comes out clean. Cool in pans on wire racks 10 minutes; remove from pans to wire racks, and cool completely.

7. Tint Vanilla Frosting with food coloring gels. Frost each cupcake with tinted frosting. (See How-To, page 23.)

baker's secret

• For a dairy-free option, you can use soy milk and shortening to replace buttermilk and butter in the cake. Omit the Vanilla Frosting, and dust the tops of each cupcake with powdered sugar.

If you are in need of a little "hot" romance, this is your cupcake. It has a mild or major kick of heat depending on how much red chile pepper you add. The combination of dark cocoa and hot pepper will light your fuse, and the red candy lips will cause the spark.

Hot Mama

makes 24 cupcakes

flip it!

Firecrackers

• Flip this recipe to create a sparkling New Year's Eve dessert. Prepare Chocolate Cake cupcakes as directed, substituting Chocolate Frosting (page 41) for the frosting. Cut red licorice candy into 2-inch pieces for firecrackers. Make fuses from string licorice strips. Place 3 firecrackers into each cupcake. Top with multicolored sprinkles.

baker's secret

• You can find the red candy lips for Hot Mama at cakedeco.com.

1 recipe Chocolate Cake (page 45)	Toppings: red candy lips, red sparkling sugar
2 recipes Spicy Dark Chocolate Frosting	

1. Prepare Chocolate Cake as directed.

2. Fill each cupcake with Spicy Dark Chocolate Frosting. (See How-To, page 21.)

3. Frost each cupcake with Spicy Dark Chocolate Frosting. (See How-To, page 23.) Top each with red candy lips and sparkling sugar.

spicy dark chocolate frosting

½	cup butter, softened	⅛	tsp. salt
½	cup dark unsweetened cocoa	1	(16-oz.) package powdered
⅓	cup whipping cream		sugar
¼	to ½ tsp. ground red pepper		

1. Beat first 5 ingredients at medium speed with an electric mixer until creamy.

2. Gradually add powdered sugar, beating at low speed until blended. Beat at high speed 2 minutes or until creamy. Makes 3 cups.

We occasionally have requests for cupcakes without frosting. So for purists who like their cake plain, this is just the thing. It's also a great New Year's resolution cupcake when you just have to have something sweet. If you want something a little more exciting than powdered sugar, top your cupcakes with a dusting of sweetened cocoa or cinnamon-sugar. Or my favorite...fresh fruit, Greek yogurt, and a drizzle of honey.

Nearly Naked

makes 24 cupcakes

1 recipe of your favorite cake flavor	3 Tbsp. powdered sugar

1. Prepare your favorite cake as directed. Let cool completely.
2. Sift powdered sugar over the top of each cupcake.

This Southern classic is one of my dad's favorite cakes. Once you start eating it, you can't stop. It has all the flavors of Christmas rolled into one sweet package.

Christmas Orange Slice

makes 30 cupcakes

1	cup butter, softened	1	cup chopped toasted pecans
2	cups sugar	1	cup sweetened shredded coconut
4	large eggs		
1	tsp. baking soda		Paper baking cups
½	cup buttermilk		Vegetable cooking spray
3½	cups all-purpose soft-wheat flour	1	cup fresh orange juice (about 2 oranges)
16	oz. candy orange slices, chopped into ¼-inch pieces	1	Tbsp. orange zest
16	oz. chopped dates	2	cups powdered sugar

1. Preheat oven to 350°.

2. Beat butter and sugar at medium speed with an electric mixer until creamy. Add eggs, 1 at a time, beating until blended after each addition.

3. Dissolve baking soda in buttermilk; add to butter mixture, beating until blended.

4. Combine flour and next 4 ingredients, stirring well. Add flour mixture to butter mixture, stirring with a wooden spoon (batter will be very stiff).

5. Place 30 paper baking cups in 3 (12-cup) muffin pans, and coat with cooking spray; spoon batter into cups, filling two-thirds full.

6. Bake for 12 to 15 minutes or until a wooden pick inserted in center comes out clean. While cupcakes bake, combine orange juice, zest, and powdered sugar, stirring until smooth.

7. Cool cupcakes in pans on wire racks 10 minutes; remove from pans to wire racks. Brush orange glaze generously over hot cupcakes. Let cool before serving.

A Dreamcakes' Christmas favorite is our Peppermint Mocha cupcake. It makes an extraordinarily beautiful cake that even Santa would love to receive!

Peppermint Mocha

makes 48 mini cupcakes

1	recipe Mocha Cake (page 88)		Toppings: snowflake sprinkles,
1	recipe Chocolate Ganache (page 39)		hard peppermint candies
1	recipe Peppermint Mocha Frosting		

1. Prepare Mocha Cake using 2 (24-cup) mini muffin pans lined with mini paper baking cups coated with cooking spray, filling each cup two-thirds full. Bake for 10 minutes or until a wooden pick inserted in center comes out clean; cool as directed.

2. Fill each cupcake with Chocolate Ganache. (See How-To, page 21.)

3. Frost each cupcake with Peppermint Mocha Frosting using metal tip no. 12. (See How-To, page 23.) Top each with snowflake sprinkles and 1 peppermint candy.

baker's secret

• If you don't have coffee extract on hand for Peppermint Mocha Frosting, substitute 2 Tbsp. instant espresso dissolved in ¼ cup hot water.

peppermint mocha frosting

1	cup butter, softened	2	tsp. coffee extract
¾	cup unsweetened cocoa	2	(16-oz.) packages powdered sugar
¼	tsp. salt		
2	tsp. peppermint extract	½	cup whipping cream, divided

1. Beat first 5 ingredients at medium speed with an electric mixer until creamy.

2. Gradually add powdered sugar alternately with ¼ cup cream, beating at low speed until blended after each addition. Add remaining ¼ cup cream, beating until blended. Beat at high speed 2 minutes or until creamy. Makes 6 cups.

When I was a little girl, my mother made these for special occasions. Don't let the unpretentious appearance fool you. These 8 simple ingredients transform into a decadent dessert that is irresistible. The middle becomes the perfect little pocket to hold sweetened whipped cream or ice cream.

Fudgy Baby Cakes

makes 24 cupcakes

6	(1-oz.) semisweet chocolate baking squares	4	large eggs
1	cup butter	2	tsp. vanilla extract
1¾	cups sugar	¼	tsp. salt
1	cup all-purpose soft-wheat flour		Paper baking cups
			Vegetable cooking spray
			Powdered sugar

1. Preheat oven to 350°.

2. Pour water to a depth of 1 inch into bottom of a double boiler over medium heat; bring to a boil. Reduce heat, and simmer; place chocolate and butter in top of double boiler over simmering water. Cook, stirring occasionally, 5 to 6 minutes or until melted. Remove mixture from heat, and cool 10 minutes.

3. Whisk together sugar, flour, and eggs in a large bowl; add chocolate mixture, stirring just until combined. Stir in vanilla and salt.

4. Place paper baking cups in 2 (12-cup) muffin pans, and coat with cooking spray; spoon batter into cups, filling two-thirds full.

5. Bake for 12 to 15 minutes. Be careful not to over bake; they should be gooey. (They will crack and sink in the middle; this is normal). Cool in pans on wire racks 10 minutes; remove from pans to wire racks, and cool completely.

6. Sift powdered sugar over the top of each cupcake.

Champagne is one of my most favorite drinks. It is the beverage of celebrations...weddings, anniversaries, birthdays, and other joyful occasions. These Pink Champagne Cupcakes are our way of proposing a toast to cupcake lovers everywhere!

Pink Champagne Cupcakes

makes 24 cupcakes

1   recipe Pink Champagne Cake
2   recipes Pink Champagne Frosting

Toppings: edible glitter, pink sprinkles

1. Prepare Pink Champagne Cake as directed.

2. Fill each cupcake with Pink Champagne Frosting. (See How-To, page 21.)

3. Insert metal tip no. 10 into a large decorating bag; fill with frosting. Pipe round bubbles of frosting to cover the top of each cupcake. Top each with edible glitter and pink sprinkles.

pink champagne cake

½   cup butter, softened
1   cup shortening
2   cups sugar
4   large eggs
2¾ cups all-purpose soft-wheat flour
2   tsp. baking powder

½   tsp. salt
1   cup pink champagne
1   tsp. clear vanilla extract
2   to 3 drops red liquid food coloring
Paper baking cups
Vegetable cooking spray

1. Preheat oven to 350°.

2. Beat butter and shortening at medium speed with an electric mixer until creamy; gradually add sugar, beating well. Add eggs, 1 at a time, beating until blended after each addition.

3. Combine flour, baking powder, and salt; add to butter mixture alternately with champagne, beginning and ending with flour mixture. Beat at low speed until blended after each addition. Stir in vanilla and food coloring.

4. Place paper baking cups in 2 (12-cup) muffin pans, and coat with cooking spray; spoon batter into cups, filling two-thirds full.

5. Bake 12 to 15 minutes or until a wooden pick inserted in center comes out clean. Cool in pans on wire racks 10 minutes; remove from pans to wire racks, and cool completely. Makes 24 cupcakes.

pink champagne frosting

½	cup butter, softened	2	drops red liquid food coloring
¼	cup whipping cream	⅛	tsp. salt
2	to 3 Tbsp. pink champagne	1	(16-oz.) package powdered
1	tsp. clear vanilla extract		sugar

1. Beat first 6 ingredients at medium speed with an electric mixer until creamy.

2. Gradually add powdered sugar, beating at low speed until blended. Beat at high speed 2 minutes or until creamy. Makes 3 cups.

baker's secret

• You can find the pink sprinkles for Pink Champagne Cupcakes at indiatree.com.

Plain Jane is, well..plain, but on purpose. For those who love simple, uncomplicated flavors, this is your cupcake. You can dress up Plain Jane with lots of fancy adornments, because it's the perfect blank canvas for any occasion and will please the most persnickety palate.

Plain Jane

makes 24 cupcakes

1   recipe White Cake (page 32)
2   recipes Vanilla Frosting
    (page 33)

Toppings: white sprinkles, white
    fondant bows (optional)

1. Prepare White Cake as directed.
2. Fill each cupcake with Vanilla Frosting. (See How-To, page 21.)
3. Frost each cupcake with Vanilla Frosting. (See How-To, page 23.) Rim edges of frosted cupcakes with white sprinkles, and top each with a white fondant bow, if desired.

baker's secret

• White fondant bows can be found at cakedeco.com.

flip it!

Anniversary Cupcakes

• To transform Plain Jane into an elegant anniversary tribute, create a border around the edge of each cupcake using silver sprinkles. Top with tiny plastic champagne glasses, which can be found at party supply stores.

The heart-shaped Palmier Cookies perched on top of our strawberry cupcakes will make your heart skip a beat. The crunchy caramelized sugar of the cookies is sure to bring a smile to the ones you love.

Pretty Palmiers

makes 24 cupcakes

1   recipe Strawberry Cake (page 34)
1½ cups strawberry jam
1   recipe Strawberry Frosting (page 42)

Palmier Cookies
White sparkling sugar

1. Prepare Strawberry Cake as directed.

2. Fill each cupcake with strawberry jam. (See How-To, page 21.)

3. Frost each cupcake with Strawberry Frosting. (See How-To, page 23.) Top each cupcake with 1 Palmier Cookie.

palmier cookies

1   cup sugar, divided
1   sheet frozen puff pastry, thawed

1. Preheat oven to 425°.

2. Sprinkle flat work surface evenly with ½ cup sugar; unfold puff pastry sheet onto prepared surface. Sprinkle with remaining ½ cup sugar, covering pastry evenly. Using rolling pin, roll dough to 13- x 13-inch square and until sugar is pressed into puff pastry on top and bottom.

3. Starting at 1 short side, roll up jelly-roll fashion, stopping in middle. Repeat with other side. Cut into 24 thin slices.

4. Place slices, cut sides up, 2 inches apart on parchment paper-lined baking sheets. Bake for 10 minutes. Turn pastries over. Bake 7 more minutes or until golden brown and glazed. Remove to wire racks, and cool completely. Store in airtight containers for up to 1 week. Makes 24 cookies.

Note: We tested with Pepperidge Farms puff pastry.

baker's secret

• Microwave thawing doesn't work well for puff pastry. For the best results, thaw frozen puff pastry in the refrigerator overnight.

Sugar and spice and everything nice, that's what this little cupcake is made of. If you like a little less heat, you might want to go light on the spices. The Browned Butter Frosting takes a little time, but it's worth the effort once you've tasted it.

Spice Cakes with Browned Butter Frosting

makes 24 cupcakes

1	recipe Spice Cake
1	recipe Browned Butter Frosting

Red sparkling sugar

1. Prepare Spice Cake as directed.
2. Frost each cupcake with Browned Butter Frosting. (See How-To, page 23.) Sprinkle each cupcake with red sparkling sugar.

spice cake

½	cup butter, softened	½	tsp. freshly grated nutmeg
1½	cups sugar	½	tsp. ground allspice
3	large eggs	¼	tsp. ground cloves
1½	cups all-purpose soft-wheat flour	½	cup buttermilk
1	tsp. baking powder	2	tsp. vanilla extract
¼	tsp. salt		Paper baking cups
1	tsp. ground cinnamon		Vegetable cooking spray

1. Preheat oven to 350°.
2. Beat butter at medium speed with an electric mixer until creamy; gradually add sugar, beating well. Add eggs, 1 at a time, beating until blended after each addition.
3. Combine flour and next 6 ingredients; add to butter mixture alternately with buttermilk, beginning and ending with flour mixture. Beat at low speed until blended after each addition. Stir in vanilla.

4. Place paper baking cups in 2 (12-cup) muffin pans, and coat with cooking spray; spoon batter into cups, filling about two-thirds full.

5. Bake for 12 to 15 minutes or until a wooden pick inserted in center comes out clean. Cool in pans on wire racks 10 minutes; remove from pans to wire racks, and cool completely. Makes 24 cupcakes.

browned butter frosting

1	cup butter	⅓	cup whipping cream
4	cups powdered sugar	1	tsp. vanilla extract
¼	tsp. salt		

1. Cook butter in a small heavy saucepan over medium heat, stirring constantly, 6 to 8 minutes or until butter turns golden brown. Remove pan from heat, and pour butter into a small bowl. Cover and chill 1 hour or until butter is cool and begins to solidify.

2. Beat butter at medium speed with an electric mixer until creamy.

3. Combine powdered sugar and salt; gradually add to butter alternately with cream, beginning and ending with powdered sugar mixture. Beat at low speed until blended after each addition. Stir in vanilla. Beat at high speed 2 minutes or until creamy. Makes 3 cups.

This cupcake is wonderful as is right from the oven. But just to gild the lily, we frost it with a rich, orange-flavored frosting and sprinkle Candied Pecans on top. It also makes an incredibly beautiful cake.

Sweet Potato Cupcakes

makes 36 cupcakes

1½ cups granulated sugar	1 tsp. baking powder
½ cup firmly packed dark brown sugar	1 tsp. baking soda
1 cup butter, softened	1½ tsp. ground cinnamon
3 large eggs	¼ tsp. ground nutmeg
2 cups mashed cooked sweet potatoes	¼ tsp. salt
1 tsp. orange zest	Paper baking cups
3 cups all-purpose soft-wheat flour	Vegetable cooking spray
	1 recipe Orange–Cream Cheese Frosting (page 189)
	Candied Pecans

1. Preheat oven to 350°.

2. Beat sugars and butter at medium speed with an electric mixer until creamy. Add eggs, 1 at a time, beating until blended after each addition. Add sweet potatoes and orange zest; beat at low speed until blended.

3. Combine flour and next 5 ingredients; add to sweet potato mixture, beating at low speed until blended.

4. Place paper baking cups in 3 (12-cup) muffin pans, and coat with cooking spray; spoon batter into cups, filling about two-thirds full.

5. Bake for 12 to 15 minutes or until a wooden pick inserted in center comes out clean. Cool in pans on wire racks 10 minutes; remove from pans to wire racks, and cool completely.

6. Split each cupcake in half, and spoon bottom half of each with 2 Tbsp. Orange–Cream Cheese Frosting. Replace top half of each cupcake, and spoon an additional 1 tsp. frosting on top. Top each with Candied Pecans.

Note: Cake flour may be substituted for the all-purpose flour.

baker's secret

• Fresh sweet potatoes always taste much better, but if you are in a rush, substitute 1 (16-oz.) can of cut sweet potatoes; drain and mash them.

• To bake this recipe as a cake, use 2 (8-inch) round cake pans coated with cooking spray. Bake at 350° for 25 to 30 minutes or until a wooden pick inserted in center comes out clean.

candied pecans

1	cup pecan halves	2	Tbsp. butter
2	Tbsp. sugar	⅛	tsp. salt

1. Heat a medium-size nonstick skillet over medium heat. Add all ingredients to skillet. Cook 3 minutes or until sugar dissolves and coats pecans, shaking pan to coat evenly. Pour pecans onto a parchment paper-lined baking sheet. Let cool. Makes 1 cup.

If you are looking for an elegant dessert to end a perfect evening but are pressed for time, this is the ideal creation. The cake and Crème Anglaise can be made ahead, and the dessert tastes amazing. We sprinkle a little sparkling sugar over the top, but fresh berries would be a brilliant complement as well.

Vanilla Bean Cupcakes with Crème Anglaise

makes 24 cupcakes

1 recipe Vanilla Bean Cake (page 126)	1 recipe Crème Anglaise
	Gold sparkling sugar (optional)

1. Prepare Vanilla Bean Cake as directed.

2. Remove paper liner from each cupcake; place each on a small serving plate. Pour 2 to 3 Tbsp. Crème Anglaise over each cupcake. Top each with gold sparkling sugar, if desired. Serve immediately.

crème anglaise

6 egg yolks	1 Tbsp. vanilla bean paste
⅓ cup sugar	¼ tsp. salt
2 cups whipping cream	

1. Whisk egg yolks and sugar in a medium bowl until blended.

2. Bring cream just to a boil in a medium-size heavy saucepan. Gradually stir one-fourth of hot cream into egg mixture. Add egg mixture to remaining hot cream in pan, stirring constantly. Cook over medium-low heat, stirring constantly, 5 minutes or until mixture reaches 160° and coats a spoon. (Do not boil.) Remove from heat; stir in vanilla bean paste and salt. Let cool. Makes 3 cups.

Note: We tested with Neilsen-Massey for the vanilla bean paste.

flip it!

Baby's 1st Birthday

• This sweet cake is just the thing to celebrate baby's big day. For this version, omit Crème Anglaise, and tint Vanilla Bean Frosting (page 37) a pale blue. Frost Vanilla Bean Cupcakes with blue frosting using metal tip no. 21, and top with white sprinkles. Place a tiny rubber duck and a single tall candle on top of each cupcake.

baker's secret

• If the Crème Anglaise mixture becomes too thick, add more whipping cream, 1 Tbsp. at a time, to thin it. Store Crème Anglaise in the refrigerator if you don't plan to use it immediately.

Vegan Cupcakes can seem a tedious endeavor, but this recipe is super simple and so satisfying. These cupcakes don't rise very much, so don't panic. The frosting here is a vanilla frosting, but you can flavor it with anything you desire...such as pureed fruits, chocolate, or nuts.

Vegan Cupcakes

makes 36 mini cupcakes

1	Tbsp. cider vinegar	½	cup canola oil
1½	cups vanilla soy milk	1	tsp. vanilla extract
2	cups all-purpose soft-wheat flour	½	tsp. almond extract
			Paper baking cups
1	cup sugar		Vegetable cooking spray
2	tsp. baking powder	1	recipe Vegan Frosting
½	tsp. baking soda		Sprinkles (optional)
½	tsp. salt		

1. Preheat oven to 350°.

2. Combine cider vinegar and soy milk in a 2-cup glass measuring cup. Let stand until curdled, about 5 minutes.

3. Whisk together flour and next 4 ingredients in a large bowl.

4. Whisk together soy milk mixture, oil, and extracts in a small bowl. Pour milk mixture into flour mixture; stir just until blended.

5. Place 36 paper baking cups in 2 (24-cup) mini muffin pans, and coat with cooking spray; spoon batter into cups, filling about two-thirds full.

6. Bake for 10 minutes or until tops spring back when lightly pressed. Cool in pans on wire racks 10 minutes; remove from pans to wire racks, and cool completely.

7. Frost each cupcake with Vegan Frosting using metal tip no. 2D. (See How-To, page 23.) Top each with sprinkles, if desired.

vegan frosting

8	Tbsp. vegan butter or vegan shortening	1	tsp. vanilla extract
¼	tsp. salt	1	(16-oz.) package powdered sugar
⅓	cup vanilla soy milk		

1. Beat first 4 ingredients at medium speed with an electric mixer until creamy.

2. Gradually add powdered sugar, beating at low speed until blended. Beat at high speed 2 minutes or until fluffy. Makes 3 cups.

Note: We tested with Earth Balance for the vegan shortening.

When we have snow in Alabama, it is a rare and magical happening. We developed White Christmas to create our own little wonderland of snow. The Peppermint–Cream Cheese Frosting gives a luscious, chilly bite and sparkling scent to this bright, frosty cupcake.

White Christmas

makes 24 cupcakes

1   recipe White Cake (page 32)
1   recipe Peppermint–Cream Cheese Frosting

Toppings: edible glitter, sugar snowflakes

1. Prepare White Cake as directed.

2. Fill each cupcake with Peppermint–Cream Cheese Frosting. (See How-To, page 21.)

3. Frost each cupcake with Peppermint–Cream Cheese Frosting using metal tip no. 12. (See How-To, page 23.) Top each with edible glitter and sugar snowflakes.

peppermint–cream cheese frosting

1   (8-oz.) package cream cheese, softened
½   cup butter, softened
2   tsp. peppermint extract

2   (16-oz.) packages powdered sugar
¼   tsp. salt

1. Beat cream cheese, butter, and peppermint extract at medium speed with an electric mixer until creamy.

2. Gradually add powdered sugar and salt, beating at low speed until blended. Beat at high speed 2 minutes or until creamy. Makes 6 cups.

flip it!

Med School Grad

• Talk about a flip! Transform snowy White Christmas into a cute and quirky homage to science. Omit the snowflakes, and frost cupcakes smooth with Peppermint-Cream Cheese Frosting. Cut a small square of black gum paste. (Look for gum paste in the cake decorating section at your local crafts store.) Pipe a hand X-ray with a tiny round tip and Vanilla Frosting. Let dry. Rim the edge of each cupcake with silver sprinkles, and top with the "X-ray."

baker's secret

• You can find edible glitter and sugar snowflakes at cakedeco.com.

New Year's Eve is one of the few holidays celebrated around the world. Why not ring in the new with cupcakes? Here's to celebrating new beginnings tastefully...

New Year's Cupcakes

makes 24 cupcakes

1   recipe Chocolate Cake (page 45)

1½   cups orange marmalade

1   recipe Chocolate Ganache (page 39)

Toppings: edible gold glitter, sprinkles, and dragées; miniature champagne glasses (for decoration only)

1. Prepare Chocolate Cake, substituting dark chocolate cocoa powder for the cocoa powder.

2. Fill each cupcake with orange marmalade. (See How-To, page 21.)

3. Frost each cupcake with Chocolate Ganache. (See How-To, page 23.) Top each with glitter stars, dragées, and champagne glasses.

Note: We tested with Hershey's Special Dark Cocoa Powder for the cocoa substitution.

flip it!

Graduation Day

• Add to the pomp and circumstance with cupcakes that pay tribute to the Grad. Omit the champagne glasses and gold dragées. Using black liquid food coloring, tint Chocolate Frosting (page 41) black to frost each cupcake. Roll the edges in gold glitter stars. Make a white diploma by rolling up a small square of white fondant; place a diploma on top of each cupcake. (Look for fondant in the cake decorating section at local crafts stores.)

Fruitcake—people either love it or hate it. Noel is our nod to this much-maligned Christmas tradition. Any dried or candied fruit will work in this recipe, but our favorite is cranberries. Try sprinkling the cranberries with Grand Marnier before stirring into the batter. Toasted pecans or walnuts make a great addition too!

Noel

makes 24 cupcakes

1   recipe Butter Cake (page 40)
1   cup dried cranberries
2   cups white chocolate morsels
2   (1-oz.) vanilla almond bark candy coating squares, melted
White sparkling sugar

1. Prepare Butter Cake batter; stir in cranberries and white chocolate morsels. Bake and cool as directed.

2. Drizzle each cupcake with melted candy coating; top each with sparkling sugar.

No mittens required for this glittery globe of goodness. Our delicate White Cake, creamy peppermint frosting, and crunchy sparkling sugar make this as fun as a snow day.

Snowballs

makes 24 cupcakes

1 recipe White Cake (page 32)
1 recipe Peppermint–Cream Cheese Frosting (page 229)
2 cups sweetened flaked coconut
2 Tbsp. peppermint syrup
Toppings: white sparkling sugar, edible glitter

1. Prepare White Cake as directed.

2. Fill each cupcake with Peppermint–Cream Cheese Frosting. (See How-To, page 21.)

3. Frost each cupcake with Peppermint–Cream Cheese Frosting. (See How-To, page 23.)

4. Toss coconut with peppermint syrup. Sprinkle each cupcake with coconut mixture. Top each with sparkling sugar and edible glitter to look like snow.

Note: We tested with Monin for the peppermint-flavored syrup.

baker's secret

• Peppermint syrup can be found in coffee shops, on the coffee aisle at your grocery store, or online.

flip it!

All Aboard

• This adorable cupcake transforms a regular day into a ride along the rails! Frost cupcake smooth with Vanilla Frosting (page 33) tinted with green food coloring gel. Using metal tip no. 3 and black frosting, pipe a train track around the border of each cupcake. Place a sugar train on top of each cupcake.

Strawberries look uncannily like hearts; that's why we named this recipe Stupid Cupid. It's one of our original Valentine's Day flavors that is requested year-round. Top one with a fresh strawberry or a chocolate dipped one—either way, it's a sweet way to say, "You have my heart."

Stupid Cupid

makes 24 cupcakes

1	recipe Strawberry Cake (page 34)	24	fresh strawberries
2	recipes Chocolate Frosting (page 41)		Toppings: chocolate jimmies, Chocolate Ganache (page 39)

1. Prepare Strawberry Cake as directed.

2. Fill each cupcake with Chocolate Frosting. (See How-To, page 21.)

3. Frost each cupcake with Chocolate Frosting using metal tip no. 2D. (See How-To, page 23.) Place 1 fresh strawberry on top of each cupcake. Top each cupcake with chocolate jimmies, and drizzle with warm Chocolate Ganache.

baker's secret

• To warm Chocolate Ganache, microwave in a microwave-safe bowl at HIGH 15 to 20 seconds.

Dreamcakes has a continuous love affair with all things chocolate—especially in morsel form. My daughter Katie created this particular cupcake, and it's a flavor that is requested all year long. You can't deny the perfect ratio of chocolate to vanilla in every bite.

flip it!
Mr. Fix It

• Here's a great treat for your favorite handyman. Omit the Chocolate Chip Heart Cookies and sprinkles. Tint Vanilla Frosting blue. Using metal tip no. 3 and green frosting, pipe a zigzag border around the edge of each cupcake. Top each with candy tools.

baker's secret

• You can find the red sprinkles for Sweet Cheeks at indiatree.com.

Sweet Cheeks

makes 24 cupcakes

1	recipe Butter Cake (page 40)	Chocolate Chip Heart Cookies
2	cups chocolate mini-morsels	Red sprinkles
1	recipe Vanilla Frosting (page 33)	

1. Prepare Butter Cake batter; stir in mini-morsels. Bake and cool as directed.

2. Frost each cupcake with Vanilla Frosting using metal tip no. 2D. (See How-To, page 23.) Top each with 1 cookie and red sprinkles.

chocolate chip heart cookies

¾	cup butter, softened	1	tsp. baking soda
¾	cup granulated sugar	½	tsp. salt
¾	cup firmly packed dark brown sugar	2	tsp. vanilla extract
2	large eggs	1	(12-oz.) package semisweet chocolate morsels
2⅓	cups all-purpose soft-wheat flour		

1. Preheat oven to 350°.

2. Beat butter and sugars at medium speed with an electric mixer until creamy. Add eggs, 1 at a time, beating until blended after each addition.

3. Combine flour, baking soda, and salt; add to butter mixture, beating until blended. Add vanilla and morsels, beating just until blended.

4. Line bottom and sides of a 13- x 9-inch pan with aluminum foil, allowing 2 to 3 inches to extend over sides; lightly grease foil. Spread cookie dough into prepared pan.

5. Bake for 30 minutes or until top is browned and a wooden pick inserted in center comes out with moist crumbs attached. Chill 1 hour or until firm.

6. Lift entire cookie from pan, using foil sides as handles. Cut out cookies with a 2-inch heart-shaped cutter. Makes 24 cookies.

Listening to music is what gets us going most mornings. We listen to all genres, depending on who brought their iPod that day. "She's a Bad Mama Jama" is the inspiration behind this cupcake. I hope eating this fabulous and funky flavor will inspire you to sing along with us.

Bad Mama Jama

makes 24 cupcakes

1   recipe Chocolate Cake
     (page 45)
2   cups raspberry jam, divided
1   recipe Chocolate Ganache
     (page 39)

Toppings: fresh raspberries, edible
          silver dragées

1. Prepare Chocolate Cake as directed.

2. Fill each cupcake using 1½ cups raspberry jam. (See How-To, page 21.)

3. Frost each cupcake with Chocolate Ganache. (See How-To, page 23.)

4. Melt remaining ½ cup raspberry jam, and drizzle over top of each cupcake. Top each with 1 raspberry and silver dragées.

Cupcakes for Sharing

At Dreamcakes our year is filled with lots of occasions to celebrate.
We find inspiration from all the things we love...a song, a character
from a book, movies. I love to use ordinary things in unusual ways
to create displays. Use what inspires you, and it's sure to be a success.

Whether it's a simple celebration at home or a carefully planned party for friends, we want to create something special no matter what the occasion. Cupcakes are an enchanting choice for any festivity. They can be the decoration, the party favor, and the most memorable part of the event.

Cupcakes for Sharing

Be Inspired

Every day at Dreamcakes, we meet with people who are planning all sorts of merrymaking. Here, we include lots of ideas and inspirations for you to choose from to decorate, display, and safely package your spectacular creations. Use the photos on these pages, or be inspired by an invitation, a photograph, or your favorite colors. Improvise using different candies, toppings, and flowers to create the look you want.

Presentation is a significant part of making cupcakes special, but it doesn't have to be elaborate. I love to look for unusual uses for ordinary things I already have, such as unique platters, plates, or pedestals of all sizes and shapes. Trays, marble slabs, glass, and even acrylics make great alternatives to the expected cupcake tier.

Plan for Success

When planning the number of cupcakes to prepare, a good rule of thumb is one regular size or two miniatures per person. I really love a combination of different-sized cupcakes grouped together. And the arrangement makes an interesting display.

I love to mix and match flavors. When deciding on flavors for a party, I keep the selection to around three flavors. People love to try each flavor, so be prepared for one cupcake per person per flavor. Labels with a description of each flavor are an easy way to let guests know exactly what they're enjoying.

Make Ahead

It's fine to make cupcakes ahead, especially since they're easiest to frost when chilled. Make the cupcakes a couple of days ahead, and freeze them, unfrosted, in an airtight container or wrapped tightly in several layers of plastic wrap. You can frost them while still frozen or slightly thawed. Remember to store cupcakes frosted with perishable frosting in the refrigerator.

Frosting can also be made ahead and stored in airtight containers in the refrigerator up to a week. This is especially helpful if you have several colors to be mixed. Colored frostings tend to develop a deeper color after mixing, so making them in advance gives you the option of adjusting to a lighter or darker color, if necessary. Frosting spreads best at room temperature, so be sure to give it time to stand after you remove it from the refrigerator.

Toppings and sprinkles stick best when applied immediately to the frosting. Most will not adhere once the frosting has dried. Flowers and cupcake picks can be added later, after you've arranged the cupcakes.

Fondant or gum paste cutouts are best when made ahead and dried. Once dried, store the cutouts between layers of parchment paper in a location that's cool and dry.

Package with Care

Packaging cupcakes is a tricky business. They absolutely cannot be stacked. Once frosted and decorated they must remain upright, and it's best if they don't touch—much like small children on a car trip.

One of the lessons we've learned at Dreamcakes is that packaging is crucial if cupcakes have to travel. Boxes with special holders keep cupcakes in place and prevent tipping, but there are many new, reusable cupcake carriers available as well. Some of these include carriers for individual cupcakes and others that can accommodate dozens. No matter which carrier you choose, decorated cupcakes must remain level at all times.

Create a Display

Visit your local crafts store for fun materials to use as interesting backdrops for your cupcakes. There are no set rules, so let your imagination run free.

1 Garden of Sweets: For a pretty springtime centerpiece, cover a block of florist foam with sheets of moss and fresh flowers. Display cupcakes on top.

2 Pretty Paper: Dress up individual cupcakes by placing them on paper doilies. This is an especially pretty decoration for a bridal shower.

3 Standing Tall: Give individual cupcakes the star treatment by placing them on elevated stands. The little wire holder shown below is just right for showing off specially decorated treats.

4 Topsy-Turvy: You'll find you have lots of choices for display pieces by turning containers, such as buckets, pots, bowls, even coffee mugs and wine glasses, upside down. Use several different heights of containers to make an interesting arrangement for the table or sideboard.

Candy Overload: Fill a plate, platter, or pedestal with a colorful mix of candies and sprinkles. Nestle cupcakes into the candies for a fabulously fun centerpiece.

Decorate for Party Favors

One of my favorite uses for cupcakes is as a party favor or as a place card that's also the dessert. Clever ideas to match a theme or an honored guest are so much fun and a great way to show off your artistic abilities. We chose *The Wizard of Oz* as an example of what you can do once you have an idea. (See page 242.) Run with it, and just have fun. The cupcakes don't all have to match, and you can make each one special and individually spectacular. Great things come in small packages.

Cupcakes are also a way to say "thank you" to clients or to treat a coworker or friend. They make a great little gift and a compelling way to send a message such as "I love you" or "Will you marry me?" We have sent many sweet messages to unsuspecting recipients.

1 Bag It: Our Caramel Corn Crunch cupcake is so yummy party guests will be tempted to take a bite immediately—so you should plan to make twice as many. That way you can bag extras in cellophane bags tied with a ribbon for take-home party favors.

2 Winter Treats: Catch a snowball and send it home as a party favor wrapped with squares of crisp red tissue paper.

Making Magic: Glass cloches make anything magical and might be my favorite way to display cupcakes. Filled with miniature delights, they are the perfect setting for a Christmas display. A whimsical elf adds to the merriment along with a few snippets of greenery and faux snow.

1 Dish It Up: A small bowl has a way of setting off individual cupcakes to their best advantage. Let guests take their party favor home in its own little dish. Small bowls and dishes can be had for a song at flea markets and tag sales.

2 Pan Cakes: Ordinary muffin pans are just the ticket for displaying and sharing cupcakes. For a party, display decorated cupcakes in the pan. It's a neat way to arrange them when you have multiples. Muffin pans also make it easy to transport cupcakes when you want to surprise someone with a special treat.

3 Anything Goes: Novelty pieces, like these small skillets, are a cute way to serve cupcakes as party favors. Grouped together on a table, they're also a clever table decoration.

Celebrations: *big and small*

Here's a visual feast of the many traditions we celebrate at Dreamcakes. Let these inspire your own designs.

First Birthdays

Milestone Birthdays

Baby Showers

Proposals

Wedding Showers

Weddings and Anniversaries

Graduations

New Year's

Mardi Gras

Valentine's Day

St. Patrick's Day

Easter

Fourth of July

Halloween

Thanksgiving

Christmas

Luncheons

Promotions

Artists

Pets

resources

Baking Supplies: Some good sources for pans, spatulas, cake decorating piping tips, and decorating bags are Ateco, atecousa.com; Wilton, wilton.com; Williams-Sonoma, williams-sonoma.com; Kitchen Krafts, kitchenkrafts.com; Beryl's Cake Decorating & Pastry Supplies, beryls.com. Williams-Sonoma and Wilton carry a wide variety of baking tools, decorating supplies, bakeware, and ingredients. Wilton products are also locally available in crafts stores, grocery stores, and party supply stores.

Boxes: Big River Packaging Company carries an excellent line of cupcake boxes and holders. See online at brpboxshop.com.

Candles, Toppers, and Molds: N.Y. Cake, nycake.com.

Cupcake Liners, Cupcake Wrappers: A huge variety of colors and styles of cupcake liners can be found at Sur la table, surlatable.com; Kitchen Krafts, kitchenkrafts.com; Wilton, wilton.com; Cupcake Creations, createcupcakes.com; Reynolds, reynoldskitchens.com.

Cupcake Pans: Check your local retailers for products from Wilton, Nordic Ware, Williams-Sonoma, or Fat Daddio.

Cupcake Picks: Etsy.com is a great source for personalized cupcake picks with literally hundreds of options to choose from. Visit etsy.com, or look at Michaels crafts stores or Hobby Lobby.

Cutters: Sugarcraft, sugarcraft.com; Kitchen Krafts, kitchenkrafts.com; Pfeil and Holing, cakedeco.com.

Dairy-Free Butter: Earth Balance, earthbalancenatural.com (also available at Whole Foods Market).

Dragées, Edible Pearls: India Tree Gourmet Spices and Specialties, indiatree.com; Wilton, wilton.com.

Edible Glitter: Wilton, wilton.com; Pfeil and Holing, cakedeco.com.

Egg-Free and Gluten-Free Ingredients: We love the gluten-free flours and egg replacer made by Bob's Red Mill, bobsredmill.com; you can also find Bob's Red Mill products in some local grocery stores.

Flavors and Extracts: All these flavorings are very high quality and produce exceptional results. Nielsen-Massey Vanillas, www.nielsenmassey.com; Bakto Flavors, baktoflavors.com; Boyajian, boyajianinc.com; LorAnn Oils, lorannoils.com.

Fondant and Gum Paste: Albert Uster Imports, auiswiss.com has very high quality gum paste and fondant. We love their white chocolate fondant; Global Sugar Art, globalsugarart.com.

Food Colors: Find highly concentrated food coloring at Pfeil and Holing, cakedeco.com; Wilton, wilton.com; Kitchen Krafts, kitchenkrafts.com. Food coloring can also be found in grocery stores and most crafts and hobby stores.

Gum Paste Flowers: For gum paste roses, sugar pansies, small blossoms, and other gum paste and sugar flowers, check out Sugarcraft, sugarcraft.com; Pfeil and Holing, cakedeco.com.

Edible Luster Spray: Luster spray gives a pearlized look to frostings. Pfeil and Holing, cakedeco.com.

Novelties for Toppers: orientaltrading.com; Party City, partycity.com; Dollar Tree stores.

Sparkling Sugars: Wilton, wilton.com; India Tree Gourmet Spices and Specialties, indiatree.com. India Tree has the most amazing line of sparkling sugars, sprinkles, and dragées.

Specialty Candies: Blair Candy, blaircandy.com; Candy Direct, candydirect.com; Candy Warehouse, candywarehouse.com; Jelly Belly Candy Company, jellybelly.com.

Specialty Molded Sugar Decorations: For a great variety of molded sugar decorations, we use Lucks, lucks.com; Pfeil and Holing, cakedeco.com; Sugarcraft, sugarcraft.com.

Sprinkles: India Tree Gourmet Spices and Specialties, indiatree.com; Kitchen Krafts, kitchenkrafts.com; Wilton, wilton.com.

metric equivalents

The recipes that appear in this cookbook use the standard U.S. method for measuring liquid and dry or solid ingredients (teaspoons, tablespoons, and cups). The information in the following charts is provided to help cooks outside the United States successfully use these recipes. All equivalents are approximate.

Metric Equivalents for Different Types of Ingredients

A standard cup measure of a dry or solid ingredient will vary in weight depending on the type of ingredient. A standard cup of liquid is the same volume for any type of liquid. Use the following chart when converting standard cup measures to grams (weight) or milliliters (volume).

Standard Cup	Fine Powder (ex. flour)	Grain (ex. rice)	Granular (ex. sugar)	Liquid Solids (ex. butter)	Liquid (ex. milk)
1	140 g	150 g	190 g	200 g	240 ml
¾	105 g	113 g	143 g	150 g	180 ml
⅔	93 g	100 g	125 g	133 g	160 ml
½	70 g	75 g	95 g	100 g	120 ml
⅓	47 g	50 g	63 g	67 g	80 ml
¼	35 g	38 g	48 g	50 g	60 ml
⅛	18 g	19 g	24 g	25 g	30 ml

Useful Equivalents for Dry Ingredients by Weight

(To convert ounces to grams, multiply the number of ounces by 30.)

1 oz	=	¹⁄₁₆ lb	=	30 g
4 oz	=	¼ lb	=	120 g
8 oz	=	½ lb	=	240 g
12 oz	=	¾ lb	=	360 g
16 oz	=	1 lb	=	480 g

Useful Equivalents for Length

(To convert inches to centimeters, multiply the number of inches by 2.5.)

1 in			=	2.5 cm		
6 in	=	½ ft	=	15 cm		
12 in	=	1 ft	=	30 cm		
36 in	=	3 ft	= 1 yd	=	90 cm		
40 in			=	100 cm	=	1 m

Useful Equivalents for Liquid Ingredients by Volume

¼ tsp					=	1 ml	
½ tsp					=	2 ml	
1 tsp					=	5 ml	
3 tsp	=	1 Tbsp		=	½ fl oz	=	15 ml
		2 Tbsp	=	⅛ cup	= 1 fl oz	=	30 ml
		4 Tbsp	=	¼ cup	= 2 fl oz	=	60 ml
		5⅓ Tbsp	=	⅓ cup	= 3 fl oz	=	80 ml
		8 Tbsp	=	½ cup	= 4 fl oz	=	120 ml
		10⅔ Tbsp	=	⅔ cup	= 5 fl oz	=	160 ml
		12 Tbsp	=	¾ cup	= 6 fl oz	=	180 ml
		16 Tbsp	=	1 cup	= 8 fl oz	=	240 ml
	1 pt	=	2 cups	= 16 fl oz	=	480 ml	
	1 qt	=	4 cups	= 32 fl oz	=	960 ml	
				33 fl oz	=	1000 ml	= 1 l

Useful Equivalents for Cooking/Oven Temperatures

	Fahrenheit	Celsius	Gas Mark
Freeze water	32° F	0° C	
Room temperature	68° F	20° C	
Boil water	212° F	100° C	
Bake	325° F	160° C	3
	350° F	180° C	4
	375° F	190° C	5
	400° F	200° C	6
	425° F	220° C	7
	450° F	230° C	8
Broil			Grill

index